Do you know...
the most
Speedy, Greedy,
Noisy
Birds
... in the World?

Bounty
Books

First published in 2009 by Bounty Books,
a division of Octopus Publishing Group Ltd.
2–4 Heron Quays, London E14 4JP

An Hachette Livre UK Company

A BROWN REFERENCE GROUP BOOK
Devised and produced by The Brown Reference Group plc,
8 Chapel Place, Rivington Street, London EC2A 3DQ
www.brownreference.com

ISBN-13: 978-0-753716-69-4

For The Brown Reference Group plc
Authors: Ann Baggaley, Leon Gray (Chapter 4)
Designer: Lynne Ross, Joan Curtis
Picture Researcher: Clare Newman
Managing Editor: Bridget Giles
Creative Director: Jeni Child
Editorial Director: Lindsey Lowe

PHOTOGRAPHIC CREDITS
Front Cover: Shutterstock: Florida Stock
Title Page: Shutterstock: John Austin
Photos.com: 8t, 70c, 61, 136, 163, 207t; **Shutterstock:** AJE 156, Galyna Andrushko 118t, John Austin 132,
Kitch Bain 123, Baleleur 35t, Marilyn Barbone 117t, Nick Biemans 111t, 122t, 183, Charlie Bishop 193,
Don Blais 39, Bob Blanchard 97t, Jessica Bopp 95, Barbara Brands 112b, Karel Broz 165, 198b, Joanne & Daniel
Bubnich Harris 142bl, Rachelle Burnside 13, Kris Butler 99, Narcisa Floricia Buxlea 64t, Goran Cakmazovic 41b,
Kenneth William Caleno 80, Tony Campbell 101br, Cartier 84t, Marek Cech 110, Ferenc Cegledi 115b, Josue Adib
Cervantes Garcia 118b, Sam Chadwick 203b, John De La Bastide 206, Ana De Susa 88t, Dainis Derica 63,
Rusty Dodson 40t, 119, EcoPrint 105, 161b, Tim Elliot 130br, Raymond Neil Farrimond 200, Julie Fine 65,
Richard Fitzer 100, Susan Flashman 49t, Florida Stock 91, 166, Caleb Foster 93b, Chris Fourie 71, 148, Henry William
Fu 16, J. Gatherum 181, Gelpi 81t, 157, 160, Eric Gevaert 59t, 90, Jeff Goldman 37, 57, 62t, Maksym Gorpenysk 84b,
Joe Gough 52, 190, David Hamman 50, Gertjan Haouijer 189b, Hazeelin Hassan 201b, Daniel Hebert 97t, 169t, John
Hemmings 116bl, Patrick Hermans 116br, Phillip Hollarnd 104, Anita Huszti 24, I Design 135, Vasily A. Ilyinsky 188,
Image Maker 149, Stephen Inglis 98, Jakez 11b, Stephan Jezek 21b, Gail Johnson 28, 33, JustASC 76b, B. H. Kang 86,
Kerioak/Christine Nichols 195, Ra'id Khalil 152, Pawel Kielpinski 159, Michael Kienetsky 111b, Iurii Konoval 107,
203t, Grigory Kubatyan 59b, Geoffrey Kuchera 121t, Nici Kuehl 129, Miguel Lagos Kushner 43, Dorothy Ka-Wai Lam
87, Jill Lang 117b, Lana Langlois 126, 178r, Hway Kiong Lim 78b, 81b, Alexandar Lotzov 154b, Dwight Lyman 78t,
Bruce MacQueen 182, 185, Carsten Medon Madsen 207b, Rob Marmion 29b, Artur Michalak 164l, Soldatenkor
Mikhail 11t, Linda Murrell 109, Sean Nel 121b, Thomas O' Neil 26, Netfalls 49b, Uwe Ohse 170, 201t, Mark William
Penny 184, Jaana Piira 112t, Inacio Pires 130bl, Maxim S. Pometun 32b, Graham Prentice 23, 44t, Vladimir Prusakov
73, Caso Pupo 32t, Matt Ragen 199b, Marlanna Raszkowska 79t, Lincoln Rogers 6, Armin Rose 8b, 42, 56, 62b,
RT Images 114, Salamanderman 92, Vladimir Sazonov 141, Jason Searle 58, Andrea Seemann 14, Kristian Sekulic 94,
Sergey I 142br, Michael Sheeham 79b, Ronald Sherwood 85, Igor Shootov 164r, Misha Shuyanov 199t, Siloto 64b,
Lori Skelton 75, 103, 134, Smeyf 12, Otmar Smit 89, Mike Smith 147, Snowleopard1 55, Steffen Foerster Photography,
38, 44b, 76t, 102, Michaela Steininger 72t, Steveg 122b, Summer 154t, Johan Swanepoel 77, 161t, Taolmor 10, 15,
Morozova Tatyana 208t, 208b, Brad Thompson 93t, Levgenilla Tikhonova 19, Nancy Tripp 21t, TT Photo 46t, 60,
Tuita55 131, Velefante 198t, Ozkan Vner 70b, Steve Weaver 48, Kevin Webb 101bl, Jerome Whittingham 29t, 35b, 72b,
Jan Martin Will 31, Wiz Data, Inc. 88b, John Wollwerth 36, Kim Worrell 115t, Wrangler 189b, Eldad Yitzhak 17, Mariko
Yuki 46b, Jarno Gonzalez Zarraonandia 171, Serg Zastavkin 196, Tim Zurowski 34, 40, 51t, 51b, 82, 169b, 178l, 187.

All artworks © The Brown Reference Group plc

Contents

CHAPTER 1
GROUND BIRDS
& FOWL

Which is the largest bird ever to have lived?

In 2006, scientists in Argentina dug up a 15-million-year-old fossil of the most gigantic bird ever known. This was the flightless terror bird, and it must have been truly terrifying. It stood about 3 metres tall and had a head nearly a metre long. Its huge, hooked beak measured approximately 45 centimetres. The terror bird could easily have swallowed a dog for dinner!

Do you know...?

Other enormous extinct birds include the elephant bird of Madagascar and the moa of New Zealand. The moa died out only a few hundred years ago. Prized for its meat, it was wiped out by hunting.

The moa (left) and the elephant bird (right) towered above humans.

Why have some birds given up flight?

Flightless birds include huge ones like the ostrich and smaller ones like the penguin. They all have wings, although sometimes very small ones. Scientists believe that these birds had flying ancestors. They would have lost the art of flying gradually, over millions of years.

By the 17th century, the flightless dodo had been wiped out by hunters.

Do you know...?

A big flightless bird can fight off predators or run away quickly whereas small ones are vulnerable. People and domestic animals, such as cats, are a flightless bird's worst enemies. One bird, the dodo, was hunted to extinction by humans.

The ancestors of the ostrich, say, may have got bigger and bigger, until they became too heavy to fly. Possibly, flightless birds evolved in places where there were no predators around to fly away from. Also, if food was in short supply, these long-ago flightless birds would have won out over the flyers. Ground birds need far less food for energy than those that fly.

Could the first birds fly?

Do you know...?

The forerunners of birds had scales, not feathers. Scales are made of the same material as feathers. Over millions of years, scales grew longer and evolved into feathers.

The earliest ancestors of birds may have lived as much as 225 million years ago. Recently, fossils of bird-like animals dating back to that time have been discovered. These creatures wouldn't have been able to fly. The best known of these 'early birds' is called *Archaeopteryx*, which lived around 150 million years ago. It had wings with long feathers, —it also had teeth and claws! Scientists are sure that *Archaeopteryx* could fly, or at least glide. However, it is unlikely that *Archaeopteryx* flew either very far or very well. Birds that were good flyers started to appear about 65 million years ago. If we could go back in time, we would see that many of them were similar to modern birds.

Archaeopteryx had claws on its wings.

Why do the cassowary's feathers look like fur?

The cassowary's dark, glossy feathers look very similar to the coat of a shaggy dog. Because the cassowary doesn't fly, the feathers are made differently from those of, say, a duck or an eagle. In birds that fly, each feather is held together by tiny hooks, called barbules. This creates a flat, smooth surface that air can flow over easily. The cassowary's feathers don't have barbules, so they hang loosely and limply. Each feather has a second feather growing at its base, which makes the plumage very thick. These unusual feathers allow the cassowary to push its way easily through the thick, prickly undergrowth of its forest home.

Do you know...?

A cassowary's wings are tiny. At the tip of each wing, there are just a few bare feather quills. These probably serve as extra body protection.

The cassowary has long, hairy plumage.

How do emus make their strange booming calls?

Emus are usually very quiet birds. They don't have a lot to say to each other and most of their days are spent alone. An emu is happy just being left to wander around in the Australian outback, which is where emus are found.

However, in the breeding season, one emu needs to find another emu. So the female makes a booming call to let the males know that she is close by. This call is produced as air in the emu's windpipe passes through a gap into a special air sac. The sac works like an echo chamber, which makes the boom very loud. It also helps to carry the sound over long distances. Male emus do not boom, but they sometimes grunt or hiss.

Female emus call to attract a mate.

Do you know...?

When emus pair up, it's the male that builds a nest, sits on the eggs and brings up the chicks. He is a protective, caring father and attacks any animal that might be a danger to his family. In fact, he even chases away the female emu!

Female ostriches have drab, brown feathers.

How fast can an ostrich run?

If an ostrich had a race with a horse, the ostrich might win. This is the fastest-running bird in the world. At top speed, an ostrich may reach over 65 km/h as it runs across the flat, open plains of Africa. Only a very few top-class racehorses can move as fast as that. Even when the ostrich isn't in such a big hurry, the bird can keep up a pace of about 50 km/h for at least half an hour.

The ostrich has long, strong legs and stands taller than an adult person. When an ostrich runs, it kicks itself forwards with its powerful, two-toed feet. With each stride, it can cover 3.5 metres of ground.

Do you know...?

People have trained ostriches to run races. The birds are strong and big enough to wear a saddle and carry a rider. Ostriches have also been taught to pull light, racing carts, known as sulkies. However, these birds are difficult to handle.

What use are an ostrich's wings?

An ostrich's wings are no good for flying. However, the bird uses them for all kinds of other purposes. Wings are important when a male ostrich goes courting. He crouches down near a female, spreads his wings wide and waves them about. If the female is impressed with this display, she lets the male know by using her own wings. She holds them down low and flutters them.

Ostriches also stretch out their wings to frighten off intruders that come onto their territories. When ostriches are bringing up their chicks, they have another clever use for their wings. A parent ostrich will lure a predator away from the chicks by moving off with drooping wings, pretending to be injured.

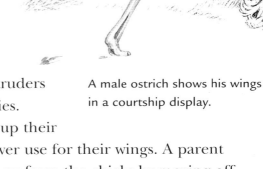

A male ostrich shows his wings in a courtship display.

Do you know...?

Ostrich plumes were once worn as fashion accessories. In the 19th century, ostrich feathers were highly popular for decorating women's hats and clothing. The first ostrich farms were set up to meet this demand. Today, ostriches are also farmed for their meat.

Which bird lays the biggest eggs?

The ostrich lays the biggest eggs, which is not surprising as it is the largest bird in the world. An ostrich egg weighs from 1–1.9 kilograms and measures up to 16 centimetres in length. The thick shell is very hard to break. Ostrich eggs are so strong that some African tribespeople use them as water pots.

To a bird as huge as the ostrich, these eggs won't look very big. But to the New Zealand kiwi, one of its own eggs must seem enormous. This little bird is no larger than a farmyard hen, but its eggs are nearly a quarter of its weight. They can measure up to 14 centimetres long. No other bird produces eggs that are so large in comparison to its size.

Do you know...?

Eggs are egg-shaped for good reasons. Being oval makes an egg easy to lay. Also, eggs that were completely round would roll about and fall from a nest. Seabirds living on high cliffs lay extra-long eggs that don't roll off.

The kiwi lays one or two eggs, sometimes many days apart.

How do cassowaries defend themselves?

The cassowary is a forest-dwelling bird found in New Guinea and Australia. It is shy and prefers to keep out of everyone's way. However, if this bird is cornered by an enemy or meets an intruder on its territory, it is very dangerous. The cassowary has a fearsome weapon. On the inner toe of each foot, it has a claw that is as long and as sharp as a dagger.

When a cassowary attacks, it leaps into the air with both feet off the ground and slashes out with these deadly claws. It is a large, powerful bird, so it can do a great deal of damage. Many humans have been killed by a cassowary, fighting its way out of a tight spot.

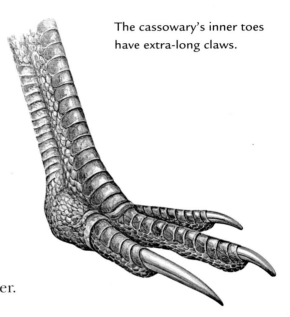

The cassowary's inner toes have extra-long claws.

Do you know...?

The dense forests where cassowaries live are getting smaller and smaller, because humans are cutting them down. When the trees disappear, it becomes harder for cassowaries to find enough food and shelter. Unless people work to save the forests, the cassowary may become extinct.

Do ostriches really bury their heads in the sand?

You may have heard the saying 'burying your head in the sand'. It means hoping that an unpleasant thing will go away if you ignore it. This saying comes from an old belief that an ostrich hides its head in the ground when danger is near. The story isn't true! Even an ostrich is clever enough to realise that simply not looking at something doesn't make it disappear.

The story may have arisen like this. When a female ostrich sits on her nest, she isn't safe. She can't run away quickly and leave the eggs for predators to eat. So she crouches down to make herself less noticeable. She sometimes puts her head flat on the ground. Perhaps people thought the bird was trying to bury her head.

The ostrich always keeps its head above ground!

Do you know...?

An ostrich's nest may contain up to 50 eggs, laid by two or more females. Although an ostrich is enormous, it cannot sit on all these eggs at once. A lot of the eggs get cold, so only about half of them hatch.

Why are kiwis nocturnal?

The kiwi's long, pointed beak is perfect for digging up worms and insects.

The word used to describe a creature that rests in the daytime and is active only at night is 'nocturnal'. The kiwi shelters in a burrow during the day and only comes out after dark to forage for food. If you were in the countryside at night, without a torch, you would find it hard to see anything. But the kiwi can see much better in the dark than it can in the daylight.

A kiwi has tiny eyes and very poor sight. In bright sunshine, it can see less than a metre ahead. At night, though, it can see nearly twice as far. Kiwis can hear well and they have a keen sense of smell.

Do you know...?

Kiwis eat all kinds of insect larvae, or grubs, which they find under dead leaves and in the soil. Their diet includes spiders, too, and they love a juicy earthworm. A kiwi also feeds on fruit and leaves.

Why does the male peacock have such an amazing tail?

The male Indian peacock has beautiful, gleaming blue feathers on his body, but it is his tail that everyone notices first. In fact, the magnificent train, with its dozens of coloured 'eyes', is not a true tail. The immensely long, fringed feathers are the outer cover of a tail made with much shorter feathers. This short tail supports the train from underneath.

The peacock's train is not just for decoration. It is there to attract the attention of the females, or peahens. In the breeding season, the peacock puts on a display by opening out his train like a fan. For added effect, he makes the fan quiver, so that all the feathers in it rustle at the same time.

A peacock's train is made for showing off.

Do you know...?

Peahens all want the male with the most 'eyes' in his train. A peacock develops more eyespots with age. A lot of 'eyes' means that the bird has survived for many years and is therefore fit and strong enough to make a good mate.

Where did the farmyard chicken come from originally?

The red jungle fowl crows at daybreak.

The domestic chickens that you see in farmyards are all descendants of wild jungle fowl. Scientists think that one bird in particular, the red jungle fowl, is most likely to be the ancestor of the farmyard chicken.

Red jungle fowl themselves are still very much alive. They are common in the forests of many countries, from Nepal and northern India to China and Indonesia. These fowl look very much like chickens and behave in similar ways. They walk about in small groups, pecking at anything that looks good to eat. The male red jungle fowl crows at dawn, just like a domestic cockerel. He is a handsome bird. His long neck feathers are bright orange or yellow and he has a glossy, greenish-black, arching tail.

Do you know...?

Humans have kept chickens for thousands of years. People in India are known to have bred chickens as far back as 3200 BC. Long ago, domestic fowl were used in religious ceremonies, often as a sacrifice, as well as for their meat and eggs.

A willow grouse changing into its winter plumage.

Why do some grouse turn white in winter?

Grouse are birds of northern countries, including northern England, Scotland, Alaska and Scandinavia. Many of them live on rugged moorlands, where the weather changes dramatically from summer to winter. Some types of grouse change their plumage with the seasons. This makes them hard to see against their background all year round and helps to keep them safe.

Do you know...?

In winter, as well as their feathers turning white, some grouse have another way of making themselves harder to see. When the snow is very deep, they dig tunnels in it and creep inside them. There they are warm and safe from any passing predators.

In summer, many grouse have reddish-brown plumage, speckled with other colours, such as black, cream and grey. This blends in with the colours of moorland plants. When winter comes, the moors are covered with deep snow. As the weather gets colder and the days shorter, the grouse shed their brown feathers and replace them with white ones. A white bird in the snow is almost invisible.

What are wattles?

Wattles are fleshy flaps of feather-free skin that some birds have under their throats or around their eyes. Chickens have them, for example, and so do pheasants. So does the cassowary. But some of the biggest and baggiest wattles belong to turkeys.

Wattles are usually brightly coloured. They are often red, but come in other colours, too. These skin flaps are normally more noticeable on male birds than on females. You might think wattles are strange things to wear on your head, but they can be very important to birds. For example, male turkeys make use of them to attract females in the breeding season.

A male turkey has impressive red wattles.

Do you know...?

A male turkey expands his wattles when he is trying to attract the attention of a female. His courting display also includes fanning out his tail feathers and shaking the flight feathers on his wings.

Can the kakapo be saved from extinction?

The kakapo is something of an oddity in the bird world. It is a parrot that cannot fly. New Zealand is the only place in the world where this very rare bird is found.

Once, the kakapos had no natural enemies and thrived all over New Zealand. Then humans came and started to hunt them. Later, settlers who arrived from Europe cut down much of the forest that the kakapos lived in. They also brought with them animals such as cats and rats, which preyed on the kakapos. By the end of the 1970s, the kakapo was almost extinct. People started working to save the kakapos, moving them to New Zealand's offshore islands. There the birds can breed in safety, but no one can yet be certain of their survival.

The kakapo is barely clinging to survival.

How was the New Zealand takahe re-discovered after scientists thought it was extinct?

The takahe is a protected bird.

It ought to be easy to see a takahe, with its bright blue and green plumage. But people hardly ever do, because the bird is very rare. By the 19th century, takahes were thought to be extinct. But in 1948, scientists discovered some still living in lonely valleys on New Zealand's South Island. Plans were immediately made to protect these remaining birds.

At what weight does a bird become too heavy to fly?

The great bustard is nearly too heavy to fly.

Do you know...?

Another heavyweight is the great bustard, which looks very much like a monster turkey. This bird only really flies when it absolutely has to. Before launching itself into the air, it makes a very long run to get up enough speed for take-off.

Scientists estimate that a bird weighing over 15 kilograms would find it impossible to take off. This is about the weight of a large swan. To fly, a swan pushes itself out of the water by pedalling madly along with its feet. A huge seabird, such as an albatross, glides effortlessly. But to get up in the air, it has to pick a time when there is a good wind. Then it launches itself into the air current.

Why is the kiwi the only bird to have nostrils at the tip of its beak?

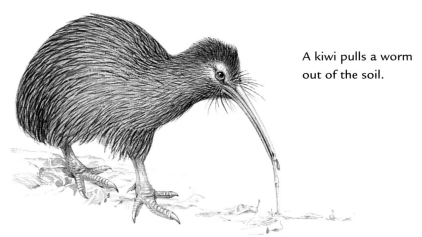

A kiwi pulls a worm out of the soil.

All birds except the kiwi have nostrils at the tops of their beaks, close to their foreheads. The kiwi's nostrils are right at the very tip of its long, narrow beak. This special arrangement helps it to find food.

The things that a kiwi eats, such as worms and grubs, are hidden under dead leaves or buried in mud. A kiwi forages around for food by using its keen sense of smell. Being able to push its nostrils down into the ground enables the bird to sniff out a tasty meal deep in the soil. A kiwi's nostrils are made with a valve to help prevent dirt getting up its nose. If the bird does sniff up any dirt, it can blow it out again with a quick snort!

Do you know...?

The kiwi has poor eyesight, but its other senses are truly excellent The bird's sense of smell is much better than that of most other birds. A kiwi also has extremely sharp hearing. Its ear openings can be seen very clearly on each side of its head.

CHAPTER 2
BIRDS OF SEA & SHORE

Which bird flies for years at a time?

Most sea and shore birds are good flyers. Gulls, terns, skimmers and skuas spend most of their time in flight. They fly long distances as the seasons and food sources change. Or, they might fly long distances to find mates and breed.

Perhaps the most amazing flyers of all, though, are young sooty terns. Before they are old enough to breed, sooty terns spend several years flying at sea. They hardly ever stop to rest on the water. Instead, they even catch their food mid-flight by skimming the sea's surface. After six to eight years of non-stop flying, a sooty tern is ready to breed and will finally come back to land.

A sooty tern is white below and black on top, except for a white forehead.

Which birds nest in burrows?

A puffin inspects its burrow.

Birds that live on sea cliffs have a problem when they want to build nests. There are no nearby trees for them to take twigs from. Some birds overcome this difficulty by nesting in burrows. Among them is the puffin.

Puffins choose breeding sites on clifftops where the soil is deep and soft. Then they start to dig. Making a burrow is hard work, but the puffin has some useful tools. It uses its big beak to delve into the earth and to carry away stones. A puffin also has strong, webbed feet to push loose soil out of the hole. A pair of puffins usually share this task.

Do you know...?

Puffins sometimes save themselves the bother of digging a burrow by moving into one that is ready made. They may use an old rabbit hole or a burrow that has been dug out by another seabird, the shearwater.

A female eider duck lines her nest with eiderdown.

Why is eiderdown so warm?

Next time you snuggle up in bed, remember to thank the ducks that might be keeping you warm! If you are lucky enough to have expensive pillows or quilts, they might have been stuffed with duck feathers, or eiderdown. Common eiders are ducks that live in cold and icy northern seas. Females pluck down from their chests to line their nests. These small and fluffy feathers trap a lot of air. The trapped air is warmed by the chicks' bodies (or yours).

Do you know...?

Eiderdown was widely used in the past. Today, eider ducks are protected and eiderdown is expensive. Down can only be collected after chicks have left the nest. Now, pillows and quilts are more likely to be stuffed with goose feathers or artifical fibres than with eiderdown.

How long can a penguin stay under water?

Penguins hurl themselves into icy waters.

All penguins are amazing divers and swimmers. They sometimes make hundreds of dives a day in search of food. If you swam under water, you would need to come up for air every few seconds. A penguin can stay down for longer.

Small penguins, such as the Adélie or gentoo, can stay under water for one to two minutes. During that time, they dive to depths ranging from 10 metres to more than 150 metres. Bigger penguins, such as the enormous emperor penguin, dive deeper, perhaps 500 metres or more. An emperor penguin's dive can last for more than 18 minutes.

Do you know...?

To stay under water without breathing, a penguin needs a store of oxygen in its body. This is because the bird's muscles need oxygen to keep working. However, muscles use less oxygen under water than they do on land.

Does anything eat penguins?

An Adélie penguin protects
its chick from a skua.

Unfortunately for
penguins, several
creatures find them good to
eat. In the sea, a penguin's
worst enemies are killer
whales, sharks and seals
such as the leopard seal.

On land, penguins must
keep a wary eye open for
flying predators. Large
seabirds, such as skuas
and giant petrels, are bold
thieves that rob penguins
of their eggs. These birds
also snatch penguin chicks
and destroy eggs, too.

Do penguins live in hot places as well as cold ones?

When we think of penguins, we imagine them living in the midst of snow and ice. Most species of penguin do, in fact, live in extremely cold places. Many are found in the Antarctic regions. There are a few penguins, though, that like to live somewhere a bit warmer.

These two are African, or jackass, penguins.

Do you know...?

At the hottest times of day, the Galápagos penguin stays in the sea. When it comes on shore, it avoids getting too hot by resting in shady spots.

Galápagos penguins are found on the tropical Galápagos Islands. These islands lie in the Pacific Ocean, off the coast of Ecuador. Here, temperatures can reach more than 40° Celsius. However, the seas around the islands are always cool because of the currents. Another penguin that prefers a mild climate is the little penguin that lives around Australia and New Zealand. There is even an African penguin. This is sometimes called the jackass penguin and it is found on the coast of South Africa.

Why doesn't the kittiwake fall off its cliff ledge?

You can fit a lot of kittiwakes on the face of a cliff. These little gulls gather on sea cliffs in tens of thousands, or even hundreds of thousands. A kittiwake colony is very crowded, very noisy and very smelly! Kittiwakes perch and build their nests on the tiniest and narrowest of ledges, at dizzy heights above the sea. But none of them ever seems to fall off.

A kittiwake has short legs which allow it to stand firmly upright on the smallest ledge. It also has long claws on its feet, which give a good grip on slippery rocks. Young kittiwakes stay in their nests much longer than other gull chicks. By the time they do leave the nest, they are ready to fly. There is no danger of them falling.

Do you know...?

Kittiwakes don't always need a cliff to nest on. A tall building with plenty of narrow window ledges is just as good. Sometimes, kittiwakes are even found nesting inland on flat rocks or sand.

The kittiwake doesn't need much room.

Why are there no penguins in the Arctic?

There are millions of penguins in the icy regions of Antarctica. So isn't it odd that there are none in the Arctic, which has the same cold climate that penguins like? The reason penguins never evolved in the north is probably because there are too many dangerous land predators there, such as polar bears, wolves and arctic foxes. However, instead of penguins, the arctic regions had another flightless bird, the great auk. Great auks have not survived. The birds were extinct by the mid-19th century. The auks' biggest enemies were not polar bears but people, who killed them in thousands for their feathers and meat.

The great auk is now extinct. Other types of auk still live in the Arctic, though.

Do you know...?

There are more than 20 types of auk, including razorbills, guillemots (right) and puffins. Auks have been called the penguins of the north. Like penguins, they stand upright and often gather in breeding colonies. They also dive deep and 'fly' under water using their wings.

Which bird has the longest migration?

E very year, the arctic tern flies nearly from the North Pole to the South Pole and back again. At the end of its mammoth round trip, the arctic tern may have covered over 40,000 kilometres! No other bird regularly makes such a journey. This elegant little seabird breeds high up in the arctic circle, where the sun never sets during the summer. Arctic terns

The arctic tern is a long-distance traveller.

nest in colonies on rocky shores and islands. At the end of the breeding season, the terns head for Antarctica at the other end of the world. When they arrive, it's summer in the Antarctic, so the birds enjoy daylight all the time there, too.

Do you know...?

The only time the arctic tern doesn't fly is when it moults its feathers. This happens after it reaches Antarctica. Until its feathers re-grow, the tern has to feed as it swims, collecting food from just under the surface of the sea.

Why do seabirds follow boats?

A shrimp boat surrounded by a flock of gulls hoping to pick up some tasty scraps.

Where there's a ship there is bound to be a trail of seabirds following in its wake. Gulls, albatrosses, petrels, gannets and many other birds are drawn to ships like iron filings to a magnet. They may enjoy riding the air currents but their main purpose is to watch for any scraps of food or edible rubbish to be thrown overboard. A cruise liner can be a good source of food, but to a seabird the very best ships to follow are fishing trawlers. Fishermen throw out a lot of waste – fish that are damaged or too small to sell – as well as the innards of fish they have gutted. Seabirds will tag behind a fishing trawler for days on the lookout for tasty treats.

Do you know...?

Seamen used to think that killing an albatross would bring bad luck. They believed that the bird held the souls of drowned seamen. But these fears didn't stop sailors regularly killing albatrosses for food!

How fast can a penguin swim?

All penguins can swim quite quickly, but the winner of the penguin Olympics has to be the gentoo penguin. This bird 'flies' along under water at a top speed of more than 25 km/h.

Penguins are designed for fast swimming. They may look clumsy waddling about on land but in water they are sleek and graceful. Their smooth, rounded bodies move through the water as effortlessly as fish. Their flippers have very strong muscles. Each flap of the flippers propels the penguin powerfully along. The penguin has broad, webbed feet that help to steer it through the water as it changes direction or dives. The penguin's stumpy tail makes a good rudder that helps to keep the bird moving in the right direction, too.

Gentoo penguins are the fastest swimmers.

Do you know...?

Every now and then a penguin needs to pop up from the sea to take a breath. Some types of penguin leap right out of the water. This action is called porpoising. Porpoises jump into the air in a similar way.

Why do puffins have such colourful beaks?

The puffin's bright beak makes this bird instantly recognisable.

Pictures of puffins nearly always show the bird's outsized beak covered in multi-coloured stripes. But for much of the time, the beak doesn't look nearly so bright. A puffin has this splendid decoration only in the breeding season to attract them to one another when they are looking for a mate.

As the breeding season approaches, nine hard, coloured plates grow over the beak. After the puffins have all paired up, laid their eggs and raised their chicks, the breeding season ends. Colourful beaks won't be needed for another year. So the plates drop off and the puffin's beak looks smaller and duller. Puffins don't develop a fully coloured beak until they are about five years old.

Do you know...?

It is not just the beak that brightens up a puffin in the breeding season. The bird's legs also change colour from dull yellow to vivid orange. For further ornamentation, small blue patches appear above and below the eyes.

Why do skimmers have 'upside-down' beaks?

Skimmers are fish-eating birds that live either along the coast or by lakes and rivers. They take their name from the way they skim low over the surface of the water. There are several types of skimmer. Black skimmers are found in North and South

No other bird has a beak like a skimmer.

America. There are also African and Indian skimmers.

These birds look a little like gulls, except for their curious beaks. The lower part of a skimmer's beak is much longer than the upper part. When a skimmer hunts for fish, it flies with its beak held wide open. The tip of the beak's lower half scoops through the water. The minute it touches a fish, the skimmer dips down its head and snaps its beak shut on its prey.

Do you know...?

Many people who fish for sport would be envious of the success rate of the skimmer. In some areas, black skimmers have been studied carefully. The skilful birds have been seen to catch one fish about every 30 seconds.

How do baby waders protect themselves?

A mother killdeer keeps her chicks safe under her wing.

Waders are birds of the seashore and marshlands. They include sandpipers, snipe, oystercatchers and plovers. All waders build their nests on the ground. That puts the chicks in great danger. They cannot fly away or even run very far if a predator turns up. Foxes, crows and gulls can easily take a chick from its nest.

Do you know...?

Wader chicks grow up quickly. Many young are able to run around and find food for themselves very soon after hatching from their eggs. Their parents keep a watchful eye and lead them to good feeding places.

Wader chicks know by instinct how to protect themselves. For example, baby lapwings, a type of plover, respond immediately if they hear their parents giving alarm calls. The chicks crouch low and stay absolutely still. Their speckled, downy feathers are very hard to see against the ground. If they 'freeze' like this there is a chance that a predator will not notice them. Other waders use this trick, too.

Why do gulls love rubbish?

Huge numbers of gulls flock round a rubbish tip.

Humans create a lot of food waste and much of it ends up on rubbish tips. Gulls, always quick to spot an opportunity, have made good use of this waste. To a seagull, a rubbish tip is as good as a free restaurant! It can have a big meal without the effort of going hunting. Until recently, because gulls thrived on such a great supply of food, their numbers kept increasing. Now that people are getting rid of their rubbish in better ways, the gulls aren't doing quite so well.

You might expect a gull to like fish more than rubbish. In fact, these birds are ready to eat almost anything. They do like fish, but they also eat small birds and mammals, and even some types of worm.

Do you know...?

Herring gulls are one of the most common types of gull, often living in towns as well as on the coast. They raid waste bins for whatever looks edible. These city slickers can be aggressive towards people, especially in defence of their nests.

Why do emperor penguins march so far over the ice to breed?

Emperor penguins nest on the sea ice that forms round the coastline of Antarctica in winter. Before they start breeding, they spend weeks at sea fattening themselves up on fish. When the ice forms it stretches far out to sea. You would think that the penguins just had to climb out of the water to find a good nesting place.

But sea ice can easily break up in the big storms that occur in an Antarctic winter. To be safe, emperor penguins make their nesting colonies as close to the coast as possible. Here, the ice is firmly fastened to the land and very solid. To reach their colonies, emperors may walk for up to 200 kilometres. Thousands of them can be seen tramping in long lines across the ice.

Emperor penguins usually mate for life. Pairs group together in large breeding colonies.

Do you know...?

To keep warm in an Antarctic blizzard, emperor penguins huddle together in tight packs. As the unlucky ones on the outside get colder, they start to shuffle their way into the middle of the crowd, where it's warmer.

Can storm petrels really walk on water?

Two storm petrels
'walk' on water.

Storm petrels are the smallest seabirds. Some are no bigger than a sparrow. Petrels spend a lot of their lives out over the oceans. They fly just above the surface of the water when they are searching for food. Often, their feet actually touch the waves and they look as though they are walking on the sea.

However, petrels cannot really walk on water. What they are doing is just dabbling their feet on the tops of the waves. They hover on their wings to stay up in the air. When petrels 'walk' they are probably using their feet to stir up the small sea creatures that they feed on. This could make it easier for the petrel to pick out its prey.

Do you know...?

Petrels may have got their name from Peter (below), a saint who was also said to walk on water. Storm petrels are so called because they have a habit of getting close to ships to shelter from storms.

43

Why do gannets live in such massive colonies?

There's no room to spare in a gannet colony.

Many thousands of gannets may occupy one breeding site. The overcrowding is just terrible! Each gannet's nest is jammed in between others and there's hardly room to move.

Gannets all agree on what makes a good site. It must be safe from predators, preferably on a small island with steep cliffs. But the right places are in short supply. If a suitable spot is found, gannets arrive from far and wide to compete for room. With so many neighbours, tempers get lost and fights break out.

Do you know...?

The gannet colony at Bass Rock, in the Firth of Forth, is one of the largest in the world. Around 140,000 gannets live there in spring and summer. Against the dark rock, their white plumage looks like a heavy fall of snow!

Which is the world's most common seabird?

The answer to this question is not as simple as you might think. No one really knows for sure which seabird is the most common because no one has actually counted them all! However, experts have a good idea which bird is probably the most common. On the cold, icy coasts of Antarctica and nearby islands, more than 50 million pairs of Wilson's storm petrels are breeding. Since each pair will produce at least one young, that makes for a population numbering far more than 100 million birds!

Do you know...?

Wilson's storm petrels make long journeys, or migrations, each year. These birds fly south for thousands of miles, from their summer homes north of the equator to their breeding sites in Antarctica. Huge flocks of several thousand Wilson's storm petrels gather at staging places to socialise and rest during this migration.

Wilson's storm petrel is about the same size as a sparrow.

What are tubenoses?

Tubenoses are exactly what their name says they are! These birds have their nostrils set in two long tubes, either on top of, or at the sides of, their beaks. The tubenoses are all ocean-going birds. They include various types, from huge albatrosses to tiny storm petrels.

Tubenoses are nearly always on the wing, far out at sea, no matter how rough the weather. They can all swim and some of them can dive, too. Most tubenoses find

A northern fulmar is a type of tubenose.

moving on land difficult. Their legs and feet are weak and just not made for walking properly. Tubenoses nest on the coast, where many of the smaller ones dig burrows for safety. The powerful albatrosses are afraid of nothing, so they nest on open ground.

Do you know...?

The strange nostrils of tubenoses may give them a good sense of smell. It is thought that they can find their own burrows in the pitch black by picking up their scents.

Why do some waders have strangely shaped beaks?

The pied avocet filters food in its beak.

Wading birds usually have to hunt for their food in water or wet, muddy places. When lunch is hard to get at, it helps to have a specially designed beak. The pied avocet has a long, slender bill that curves upwards. The bird sweeps its open beak through water like a scythe. When it lifts its beak, the water drains away but all kinds of food is left behind. A curlew's beak is also long and thin, but it curves downwards. The curlew stabs its beak deep into mud. Sense organs on the beak's tip locate prey. Perhaps the weirdest wader beak is that of the rare spoon-billed sandpiper. The two halves look exactly like a pair of spoons.

Do you know...?

The wrybill of New Zealand seems an ordinary bird. But look closer! The wrybill's beak bends to the right in a very odd way. It is used for probing under pebbles and scooping up food from the mud.

How do seabirds avoid taking in too much salt?

Do you know...?

The Maoris of New Zealand believed that the salty fluid running down an albatross's nose was tears. In one version of the legend, the albatross was thought to be crying for a lost love. In another version, the bird weeps because it longs to fly away from land and back to the ocean.

A lot of the things that seabirds eat, such as fish and other marine food, are full of salt. Too much salt is unhealthy, so the birds have to get rid of some of this salt.

All seabirds have certain glands close to their nostrils. These glands very quickly remove much of the salt from the birds' diet. The unwanted salt is contained in a fluid that runs out of the birds' nostrils.

An albatross has salt glands in its nose.

Why do cormorants air-dry their wings?

Cormorants spend a great deal of time in the water. They are great fishers and divers. Unlike other water birds, such as ducks, a cormorant's feathers are not very waterproof. Nor does its plumage trap air bubbles, which is what keeps a duck bobbing on the surface of the water and stops it from sinking. A lack of air bubbles helps the cormorant to dive, but it does also mean that the bird swims low in the water. Also, without having air trapped against its body, the cormorant loses heat quickly. So when it gets out of the water, a cormorant feels really cold and wet. That is why these birds sit on rocks or tree stumps with their wings held out wide. They are drying off and warming up.

A cormorant spreads its wings to air-dry.

Do you know...?

When it is time to breed, the dull plumage of cormorants is brightened up by brightly coloured patches of skin on the face and feathered crests.

How do parent penguins recognise their own chicks in a crowd?

Penguin breeding colonies may contain hundreds of thousands of birds. Many of these are chicks. As soon as the chicks are old enough to be left alone, the parents go off to find food for them. The chicks gather together in a 'nursery', which is known as a crèche. When the parents return, the youngsters all greet them eagerly, begging to be fed. First, the parents have to find their own chicks among the vast hungry throng. It seems an impossible task. The chicks all look alike!

Do you know...?

Some unlucky penguin chicks lose both their parents to predators. To survive, these orphans may elbow their way into someone else's nest and get fed along with the resident chicks.

To attract attention, penguin chicks make a whistling noise. Just as we recognise a person's voice, so parent penguins know their own chick's whistle when they hear it. They locate the sound and track down the waiting chick.

Fluffy penguin chicks wait for their parents.

Why do dunlins chase the tide?

Dunlins find food as the tide goes out.

Dunlins often breed inland but for the rest of the year they prefer to be in coastal areas. In winter, they gather in thousands on sandy beaches or the mudflats of tidal rivers.

Dunlins feed on the worms, snails and small shellfish found in the mud or sand. When the tide is out, wide feeding areas are uncovered. The dunlin flocks spread out and concentrate on eating. The birds thrust their beaks into the mud to search for tasty morsels. As the tide creeps back in, the dunlins, still eating, get crowded together in an ever-shrinking space. Eventually, their feeding ground is completely covered in water. The dunlins give up and go inland to wait for the tide to turn again.

Do you know...?

The way dunlins feed is sometimes referred to as stitching. Dunlins poke their beaks into the mud up to a hundred times a minute. They do this poking so fast that their beaks look like sewing-machine needles whizzing in and out of cloth.

A dunlin in its breeding plumage.

Why are sand eels so important for seabirds?

A puffin can pack a lot of sand eels into its beak.

Sand eels are not actually eels but small fish. They burrow into the sandy bottom of the sea and swim up to feed. Seabirds, including puffins, kittiwakes and many others, rely on sand eels as one of their main sources of food. The fish are very nourishing so they are ideal for feeding to young chicks. Some parent seabirds feed their chicks on almost nothing else until the young are ready to fend for themselves. In recent years, the numbers of sand eels have been falling, possibly because the waters they live in are getting warmer than they like. This leaves seabirds short of their favourite food, and many are not breeding very well.

Do you know...?

Sand-eel fishing is important to people, too, and the fish are caught in huge numbers. To make sure that seabirds get enough sand eels, some countries have agreed to stop fishing so heavily.

Why do albatrosses mate for life?

Albatrosses live for a long time, sometimes up to 30 years. They are late starters at breeding and may be halfway through their lives before they find a mate. Albatrosses breed only every other year, so they are slow to reproduce. To make things even slower, albatrosses take quite a long time to choose a mate. The birds go through complicated courtship rituals.

The albatross is a faithful mate.

When two albatrosses pair up, it makes sense for them to stay together for life. Then they don't have to start all over again. If an albatross loses its mate, it could wait years before finding another suitable partner. And that would mean fewer chicks being produced.

Do you know...?

If two albatrosses are attracted to one another, they perform a courtship display. This looks very much like a dance. The pair circle round and round, stretch out their wings, point their heads in the air and rattle their beaks.

How do pelicans catch fish?

Pelicans look amusing with their big, clumsy bodies and enormous throat pouches. They are clever, though, especially at catching fish. Most pelicans feed as they swim along. A pelican simply sticks its head under water and if it finds a fish, it neatly scoops it into its pouch. Some types of pelican form fishing parties. Several birds line up in a row and drive the fish into shallow water. Then everyone gathers round to share an easily caught meal.

The brown pelican has a hunting method that is not used by any other pelican. It flies over the water looking for fish. When it spies prey, it dives down into the water head first, making a colossal splash.

Do you know...?

The pouch that a pelican has attached to the lower half of its bill is very elastic. As the pelican fills this pouch with fish, it stretches. The bigger types of pelican can hold over 12 kilograms of fish in their pouches.

A brown pelican dives head first into the water.

Which seabird is like a flying pirate?

One frigatebird attacks another in mid-air to steal its food.

Pirates once sailed the seas, attacking and stealing from boats laden with valuable goods. While there are not many human pirates around any more, some seabirds act like pirates by stealing food from other birds. Some of these pirates attack other birds while they are on the ground or on the sea. But frigatebirds are the pirates of the air. They chase their victims in the air and bully them into giving up their hard-won prey. If chasing isn't enough, the frigatebird uses its hooked beak to grab a feather and unbalance its victim in the air.

Do you know...?

Frigatebirds have long been familiar to sailors. These birds often follow ships and fight over any scraps of food they can seize. Sailors named these pirate-like birds frigatebirds or man-o'-war birds after the fast, well-armed ships used by real pirates.

Which bird has the largest wingspan?

It's the wandering albatross that goes into the record books as the bird with the greatest wingspan. The biggest one known so far measured a terrific 3.7 metres from wingtip to wingtip. Albatrosses are massive seabirds that stay in the air for days. They cruise over the oceans with the wind and hardly have to flap their wings at all. The bird that comes second to the albatross is not a seabird but a condor, which is a type of vulture. An Andean condor can have a wingspan of up to 3 metres.

Do you know...?

The bird with the biggest wingspan ever lived six million years ago, and has long been extinct. This bird, known only by its scientific name, *Argentavis magnificens*, had a wingspan of about 7 metres. Even an albatross would look small beside that!

Many albatrosses have a wingspan of more than 3 metres.

Why are the nests in Adélie penguin colonies so evenly spaced?

An Adélie penguin colony is a very crowded place. But the nests are carefully sited at regular distances from each other. Each pair of penguins has just enough personal space to sit on eggs and tend to chicks. There's no room to spare, though! If penguins stretch out their necks they can touch beaks with the birds nearest to them.

Life in a penguin colony is never lonely.

Do you know...?

Adélie penguins use mostly pebbles or small stones to build their nests. Shuffling around collecting one pebble at a time is hard work. To save themselves a bit of time and effort, the penguins are not above stealing a pebble or two from each other's nests.

This might be a bit close for real comfort but it also makes things difficult for predators. A predator, such as a skua, sneaking up to rob a nest while the parents' backs are turned, has to watch out for the next-door neighbours. An intruder in the colony is usually well within reach of several beaks and is likely to get a good pecking.

Gannets can spot fish from high in the air.

How does a gannet dive for fish?

A gannet hunting for food flies high over the sea. The bird has very sharp vision. It can pinpoint a shoal of fish from as high as 40 metres up in the air. When it has pinpointed its prey, the gannet plunges straight down in a superb dive. As it nears the water, the gannet draws back its wings. This reduces drag, because the streamlined body enters the waves like a spear.

A gannet has air sacs under the skin of its head, neck and breast. These lessen the impact as the bird hits the water. For further protection, see-through skin closes over the gannet's eyes. Flaps close off the nostrils to stop the bird from getting a noseful of water.

Do you know...?

When a gannet has caught a fish, it usually swallows it hurriedly under the water. This prevents another gannet from snatching its meal. Gannets are not always very polite and sometimes quarrel over food!

What do penguins use to build nests?

A jackass penguin goes nest-building.

At nest-building time, penguins have to make the best of what few materials they can find. On the bleak shorelines where many penguins live, there are at least plenty of pebbles around. Some penguins, such as the rockhopper penguin, start making nests by scraping out a shallow hole in the ground. They then line the hole with small stones. Others, including the chinstrap penguin, build a little platform with stones, leaving a dip in the middle for the eggs.

For a touch of added comfort and luxury, penguins often place scraps of plants, or a few feathers and small bones, inside their nests. The chicks of these penguins are the lucky ones. Some types of penguin don't build nests at all.

Do you know...?

The two biggest penguins, the emperor and king penguins, never build nests. The female lays her single egg straight onto the bare ice. Then the male steps in and moves the egg onto his feet with his beak.

How do fulmars deal with predators?

The fulmar has a nasty surprise for predators.

The fulmar looks like a gull but it is actually a tubenose. This means the fulmar is more closely related to albatrosses than to gulls. It is not a good idea to annoy or frighten a fulmar! This bird has a very effective, and quite disgusting, way of dealing with its enemies. Fulmars produce a foul-smelling oil in their stomachs. If a predator, such as a fox or a bird of prey, threatens a fulmar, it vomits out this oil with great force. The predator gets drenched and is more than likely to beat a hasty retreat. Few hunters would feel like making a meal of the fulmar after that. The oil not only smells really awful, it can damage a predator's fur or feathers.

Do you know...?

Occasionally, an unlucky person gets in the line of fire when a fulmar vomits. The victim soon finds out that the smell is difficult to get rid of. Even after thorough washing, clothes still stink!

Why don't emperor penguin eggs freeze?

The egg of an emperor penguin has a cold start in life. It is laid on ice in the depths of an Antarctic winter. An egg needs warmth if the chick is to develop and hatch out. The emperor penguin must act quickly to stop its egg from freezing.

The moment the egg arrives, the male emperor penguin tucks it snugly between his feet and his body. In the breeding season, the penguin develops a bare patch on his belly. This patch is just the right size and in just the right place for the egg to rest against. The heat of the bird's body keeps the egg nice and warm. For extra cosiness, a loose fold of the penguin's belly flops down over the egg.

Do you know...?

Like all penguins, the emperor penguin has an efficient heating system. Warm blood circulating from the centre of the bird's body passes close to the veins carrying cooled blood from the feet and flippers. This warms up the cool blood before it circulates again.

There's a warm place for an egg under an emperor penguin's belly.

Why do penguins waddle as they walk?

Penguins have extremely short legs and rather large feet, so they can't take long strides. To make walking more difficult, the legs are set far back on the penguin's body. Now think of the fat body perched upright on top of these peculiar legs! No wonder all a penguin can do is shuffle along in an odd, waddling gait.

Emperor penguins waddle in a line.

Do you know...?

Penguins on the march often speed things up by going tobogganing. If the ice is flat, they flop on to their bellies and 'row' themselves along with their flippers. It's something they all seem to enjoy!

Despite this clumsy way of walking, however, many penguins trek tirelessly across the ice over great distances.

The smaller types of penguin sometimes hop along. They can move a lot faster this way. One penguin is actually called the rockhopper penguin. This bird is good at bouncing about, with both feet together, over rocky ground.

CHAPTER 3
FRESHWATER BIRDS

Why are ducklings so fluffy?

A duckling's fluffy covering keeps it both warm and afloat in the water.

Do you know...?

The young of most ducks spend very little time in warm nests. Many ducklings join their parents in the water just a day or two after they hatch. They are able to feed themselves, too.

Ducklings need their fluffy down for warmth. Small birds lose heat from their bodies very quickly. They must constantly maintain their body heat by feeding. But without a warm covering, a small duckling swimming in cold water could rapidly become chilled and unable to feed. The fluff helps to trap warmth in the bird's tiny body, ensuring that it has enough energy to keep going. Light, fluffy down also helps to hold ducklings up in the water, so that they can bob about on the surface. Ducklings usually change from having down to feathers in a just couple of months.

Why are flamingos pink?

The flamingo is just about the pinkest bird you will ever see. Most of its feathers are pink, except the ones on its beautiful wings, which are crimson and black. Its big, curvy beak is pink with a black tip. And its long legs are very pink indeed.

The most extraordinary thing about the flamingo is that it gets its colour from the food it eats. A flamingo feeds in lakes and lagoons. It collects a beakful of water, which runs out through the sides of its beak. Tiny aquatic animals and algae are left behind for the flamingo to swallow. This food contains chemicals that are called carotenoids, because they are like the chemicals found in carrots. The carotenoids turn the flamingo pink.

The flamingo's food turns the bird pink.

Do you know...?

When flamingos are kept in captivity, their wonderful pink colouring fades if they are not given the right things to eat. Fortunately, zoos now realise this. They add supplements to the flamingos' diet so that the birds remain pink.

How are hand-reared whooping cranes taught to migrate?

A whooping crane
with its chick.

In America, there are several centres where rare whooping crane chicks are hand-reared. The aim is to release these captive birds back into the wild. Cranes are migratory. They spend the summer in one area and fly elsewhere for the winter. Wild cranes learn the routes from their parents. Hand-reared cranes are sometimes put with a flock of wild cranes, who show them the way. In another method, people teach young cranes to fly along the right route behind a light aircraft. The pilot wears a crane costume!

Do you know...?

When they are migrating, whooping cranes have been recorded flying as far as 800 kilometres in one day. Along the route, the cranes take regular breaks in their journey to feed and rest for a while.

Why do water birds have webbed feet?

Webbed feet give water birds a lot of paddling power.

Many water birds have specially designed feet that help to propel them through the water. They have three toes that point forwards and one that points backwards. The three front toes, which are usually quite long, are joined together by webbing.

Do you know...?

Water birds, such as ducks and geese, waddle rather awkwardly on land. This is because their legs are set a long way back on their bodies. The arrangement gives greater power for swimming, but it makes walking gracefully just impossible.

This is a material like tough skin. When a water bird thrusts its feet in the water, these webbed toes act as paddles. They push powerfully against the resistance of the water and send the bird skimming along. Toes without any webbing would not work nearly so well. Webbed feet are brilliant for diving, too. Some water birds plunge under water to feed. They push themselves down by using their feet in the same way as people who go scuba diving or snorkelling use flippers.

Why do killdeers pretend to be injured?

Faking it! This killdeer is trying to fool a predator.

The killdeer is a type of American plover. Like many other plovers, it nests on the ground in open places. Until the killdeer chicks have learned to fly, they are at great risk both from land predators and nest-robbing birds, such as large gulls, in the air. The chicks are hard to see, as their feathers blend in well with their surroundings. However, if a predator comes too close, a parent killdeer goes into action. To draw a predator away from the nest, the parent bird drags itself along with a wing flapping helplessly as if broken. But before the predator can pounce on this easy meal, the 'injured' bird makes an instant recovery and flies away.

Do you know...?

Some types of plover fight to save their chicks. The blacksmith plover of Africa dives down on predators from the air, making loud calls. Golden plovers do not hesitate to make angry attacks on thieving gulls.

Why do so many waders migrate to polar regions to breed?

Migratory birds travel each year between a summer breeding site and a place where they spend the winter. Many wading birds, such as some of the plovers, breed in the bleak Arctic regions, known as the tundra. For a short time in the Arctic summer, the tundra comes alive with plants, insects and other animals. That provides the breeding birds with plenty of food. But because the conditions in the tundra are still too harsh for many birds, the waders don't have to face too much competition for food and nesting sites.

The male red phalarope looks after the eggs.

The American golden plover travels from South America to breed in the Arctic.

Do you know...?

The red phalarope is one of many types of wader that nests in the tundra. When the female has laid her eggs, she flies off and leaves the male to look after them and raise the chicks all by himself. Meanwhile, the female tries to find another mate, so that she can produce another clutch of eggs.

How were great crested grebes involved with the start of bird conservation?

The feathers and skin of the great crested grebe were once much in demand for decorating ladies' clothing, especially hats. So many grebes were caught and killed, that by the mid-19th century the bird was almost extinct in Britain. To stop this cruel trade and to save the grebes, a society was formed, called the Royal Society for the Protection of Birds. Today, the great crested grebe is still scarce, although its numbers have increased. The RSPB is now one of the best-known bird conservation organisations in the world.

Do you know...?

The Audubon Society is another bird conservation organisation. It is named after John James Audubon (1785–1851), a naturalist who became famous for his paintings of North American birds.

The great crested grebe has wonderful head feathers during the breeding season.

Is a plover the same as a lapwing?

At one time, the names were often used to refer to exactly the same type of wading bird. Bird scientists have now tried to sort them all out a bit. Put very simply, the larger members of this big family of birds are usually known as lapwings and the smaller ones as plovers. The name 'lapwing' was originally a description of the birds' flight. Lapwings have broad wings with rounded tips and they fly with a slow, flapping beat. Eurasian lapwings are commonly seen on farmland in Britain. They are recognised easily by their greeny-black and white plumage.

The yellow-wattled lapwing comes from Asia.

Do you know...?

The blacksmith plover's black and white plumage is very noticeable to predators. Because brightly patterned birds often taste unpleasant, this plover's colours can actually warn predators to stay away. But this doesn't always prevent the birds from being attacked!

71

Why do geese make great sentries?

Geese make excellent watchdogs!

Do you know...?

According to legend, in 390 BC geese saved Rome from an attack by the Gauls. As the Gauls tried to creep into the city unnoticed, geese kept in the temple saw them and made a noise that raised the alarm.

It is natural for a flock of geese to be on the lookout for possible danger. When they are on the ground and feeding, they remain alert all the time. If they are disturbed by an intruder, they immediately set up a huge racket, by hissing and honking very loudly. Anyone trespassing on land where domestic geese are kept would find it hard to avoid triggering their alarm calls. What is more, a trespasser would be unable to quieten the birds down, because geese don't respond well to orders from stangers. Geese do not usually attack people, but they might give chase and can be very aggressive. They are sometimes kept instead of guard dogs to protect property.

Do swans mate for life?

Yes, they do! Once two swans have formed a partnership, they nearly always stay together for the rest of their lives. It is very rare for a swan to abandon one mate and go in search of another. Both the male and the female share the task of building the huge nest. When the eggs have been laid, usually it is the female that sits on them, while the male keeps guard close by. Once the cygnets, as young swans are known, have hatched out, both their parents take a part in the job of looking after them.

Swans form life-long pair bonds.

A breeding plumage of the great
crested grebe is very striking.

Why do grebes dance together?

Dancing is a grebe's way of getting engaged to a prospective mate. These birds have spectacular courtship ceremonies, all performed on water. When a pair first meet, there is likely to be a lot of wing spreading and feather display. Great crested grebes have ruffs of feathers on their heads, which they open out like a fan.

As the courtship 'dance' gets going, the couple may rear out of the water. Facing each other, they shake their heads from side to side. Courtship among North America's western grebes includes an astonishing performance called 'rushing'. The birds lift their bodies almost upright. They arch their necks and point their beaks upwards and, side by side, they run swiftly across the water.

Do you know...?

Part of the courtship dance of great crested grebes is a gift-giving ritual. Usually, both birds dive under the water at the same time. They each come to the surface with a beakful of waterweed, which they then shake about as an offering.

How do wood storks catch fish?

The wood stork's diet consists mainly of fish. To be sure of catching its prey, the bird has developed an almost foolproof way of fishing. Wood storks live in wetland areas, such as swamps and mangroves. The water here is shallow and usually muddy and full of weeds. In this murky water, it is hard for the stork to see its prey. It has to find fish by its sense of touch.

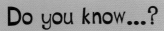

The wood stork has no feathers on its head.

Do you know...?

Wood storks have been timed to see how quickly they can catch fish. From first touching a fish to the final snap of the beak takes just 25 milliseconds. This is one of the fastest manoeuvres in the whole animal world.

A wood stork out fishing steps slowly along, with its beak pointing down into the water. It keeps its beak open and swishes it gently from side to side. The very second that the stork touches a fish it makes a rapid snap with its jaws. The sharp edges of the beak then close tightly around the unlucky prey.

How do flamingos feed?

The way a flamingo feeds is very unusual. It holds its head upside down! Flamingos wade through the water in groups, while feeding. As they move, all with their heads the wrong way up, they suck in beakfuls of water and mud. After sucking in the water, they then force it out again. They do this sucking and forcing out over and over again, very rapidly. The action may be repeated as much as three or four times a second.

A flamingo's beak is lined with fringe-like little structures that act as a filter. As the flamingo empties the water from its beak, tiny aquatic creatures in the water, such as insects, are trapped inside by the filter. These creatures are the flamingo's food.

Eating upside down.

Do you know...?

A flamingo draws water into its beak and forces it out again by using its tongue. The tongue moves backwards and forwards like a piston. Several thousand years ago, the Romans used to eat flamingo tongues, which they regarded as a great treat.

Why do jacanas have such big feet?

An African jacana walks on floating leaves.

Jacanas are found in swamps and marshes that are covered with water plants. Another name for the jacana is 'lily-trotter'. This is because the jacana often walks on the leaves of floating plants, including water-lilies. It is able to do this because of its remarkable feet.

Most jacanas are small. But they have huge feet for their size. The bird's toes are long and splayed out, covering a large area. When a jacana steps on a lily pad or other floating leaf, its weight is spread over its widely spaced toes. This stops any leaves it is on from being pushed down into the water. And the jacana doesn't sink!

Do you know...?

Moorhens are another type of bird with big feet. They spend a lot of their time swimming. However, unlike many water birds, moorhens have unusually long toes that enable them to walk easily and to even climb into bushes.

What is dabbling?

Bottoms up! A duck goes dabbling.

Take a walk around a duckpond and you will probably see a lot of feathery bottoms sticking up out of the water! These belong to ducks that are dabbling. This means that they are feeding by fishing around with their beaks for underwater plants, insects and other tasty bits and pieces. They prefer to feed in fairly shallow water. Often, ducks dabble just by dipping their beaks a little way under the water. They can pick up plenty of food like this. But to reach food deeper below the surface, the ducks flip themselves upside down. They don't stay this way for very long. After a few seconds, a duck bobs back the right way up. Young ducklings sometimes go completely under the water.

Do you know...?

A dabbling duck doesn't usually stop to pick and choose food. It takes in beakfuls of water and uses its tongue to pump the water out again. Tiny comb-like teeth on the sides of the duck's beak trap scraps of food.

What do geese eat?

Geese are birds called 'grazers'. This means that they feed mainly on grass and other green plants, just like horses and cows do. Huge flocks of geese can be seen on farmland, grazing as they

wander about. Farmers don't like geese much, because they often eat growing crops. Geese commonly go foraging in fields where crops have been harvested. Here they find rich pickings, such as spilled grain and potatoes that have been ploughed up. Geese also spend a lot of time on water and feed there, too. Sometimes they dabble, like ducks do, to reach aquatic plants.

These young geese are making a good meal of the grass.

Do you know...?

The digestive system of a goose isn't very efficient at breaking down plant food. To help grind up their food, geese swallow small pieces of grit, which they store in a part of their stomach called the gizzard.

Why do swans hiss?

A swan has big wings and will use them in an attack.

If you hear a swan hiss, you should get out of its way very quickly! This noise means the bird is annoyed. An angry swan is dangerous. It can break a person's arm with a blow from its big wings. Swans look peaceful, drifting on the water with their gracefully arched necks. But they turn fierce when they think someone is trespassing on their territory or is likely to threaten their young. A swan will step out of the water to attack. So you wouldn't be safe standing on the edge of a pond if a swan really wants to chase and attack you.

Do you know...?

As well as hissing, an angry swan puts on a threat display to frighten off intruders or rivals. It raises its enormous wings and holds them up like billowing sails. The display makes the swan look huge and scary.

Why does water run off a duck's back?

No matter how much time a duck spends in the water, its feathers never get wet and soggy. Watch a duck on a pond, bobbing or diving, or just splashing about. You can see the water running off its back like little beads. The duck sometimes gives its head or wings a shake, scattering droplets everywhere. Then the bird looks as dry as any land bird. Ducks and other water birds have a way of

Ducks waterproof their feathers with oil.

waterproofing their feathers. They have glands at the base of their tails that produce oil. A duck uses its beak to spread the oil over its feathers. This oil keeps out the water. Every feather must be coated, so ducks spend many hours at the task.

Do you know...?

Ducks and other water birds sometimes use preening actions as a way of communicating. For example, preening breast and wing feathers can be part of a ritual when two birds meet.

How do dippers walk under water?

The American dipper lives near mountain streams.

Dippers not only swim and dive, they also walk along the bottom of streams or rivers. They do this to hunt for fish or water insects. These birds have some remarkable features that protect them under water. For one thing, they have extremely thick plumage. Between the top feathers there is fluffy down. This kind of plumage acts like a padded anorak, keeping the dipper warm. The dipper also waterproofs its feathers with oil taken from the base of its tail. When a dipper is under water, its body adapts to use up less oxygen. Spare oxygen in the bird's blood keeps it going, without it having to breathe.

Do you know...?

In water, dippers blink down a transparent skin over their eyes and close their nostrils with a flap. They can actually alter their eyesight to see more clearly under water.

Why do cranes dance?

At the beginning of the breeding season, when cranes are thinking about mating, they put on a wonderful dancing display. When they dance, two cranes usually start by strutting round and round, bowing politely to one

another. Then one bird, often the male, tries a few jumps. Soon the other bird joins in. As things hot up, the movements of the cranes become wilder and wilder. They run and leap high into the air, kicking their legs. They open their wings to show off their long flight feathers. Once one couple has started to dance, the rest of the flock catches the excitement. Soon all the birds join in and in no time there is a crane disco in full swing!

Two black crowned cranes dance together.

Why do herons nest in large groups?

Two herons keep a lookout from the top of a tree.

Most herons gather together in big groups, or colonies, to feed and breed. A colony probably starts when a few herons find a good food supply. The message gets around and more and more birds arrive at the site. Herons can enjoy greater safety in numbers, with many birds on the lookout for danger. Another bonus with big groups is that the herons get a wider choice of mates.

Do you know...?

A heron colony may number about 50 or so birds. Sometimes, however, many different types of heron gather at one site. The largest mixed heron colony ever known was in the Everglades in Florida, where over a million birds were recorded living together in 1934.

Can the Hawaiian goose be saved from extinction?

The Hawaiian goose is very scarce in the wild, despite conservation efforts.

By the middle of the 20th century, there were only about 30 Hawaiian geese in existence. This goose, the official state bird of Hawaii, had not only been hunted and shot at, it had almost been wiped out by predators brought to the islands by people. Cats, dogs and mongooses had all taken their toll on the bird. To try and save them, Hawaiian geese were bred in captivity and numbers of them are released regularly into the wild. This has prevented the birds from disappearing altogether. However, the captive-bred birds do not breed very well in the wild, so numbers of wild birds are still low.

Do you know...?

The Hawaiian goose, also called the nene, is now strictly protected. Unfortunately, poachers still take the birds illegally. And every year, many of the geese are killed by road traffic.

Are male ducks always more colourful than the females?

Do you know...?

Bright plumage in male ducks is meant to catch the eye of the females. To go with their flashy feathers, some males also have highly coloured beaks. The brighter a male's beak is, the more females seem to like it!

The male mandarin duck is a vivid patchwork of different colours.

It's usually very easy to tell a male duck, or drake, from a female. The males are the ones with the fancy feathers while the females are often quite drab. However, once a year, after breeding is over, the males lose their bright plumage. For a few weeks in the summer, male ducks can be nearly as dull coloured as the females, so it is harder to tell them apart. During this moulting period, called the 'eclipse', the ducks cannot fly.

Why do baby geese follow the first thing they see?

These goslings have a parent goose to follow.

Soon after young geese, or goslings, hatch out of their eggs, they learn to follow any large moving object that they see as a parent. If the 'parent' makes noises, that gives the goslings even more encouragement to follow. However, the object might not be a parent goose. It could just as easily be a person! This learning is called 'imprinting'. It is a natural process that is designed to attach the young geese to something or someone that is likely to protect them. Once imprinting has taken place, the goslings follow the parent figure everywhere.

Do you know...?

The first person to describe imprinting, in 1935, was an Austrian zoologist called Konrad Lorenz. He made many studies of natural behaviour in animals.

Why do geese fly in a V-formation?

On a long flight, geese keep in a V-formation.

When you are out of doors, you may hear a honking sound, high up in the sky. Look up – you will see a flock of geese flying in a perfect V-formation. Geese fly like this when they travel long distances. The formation helps them to keep on flying without getting exhausted quickly. The leader, usually one of the more experienced birds, faces the most air resistance. Because other birds fly behind the leader, they meet less air resistance and don't have to try so hard. Eventually, of course, the leader starts to tire. Then another bird takes over for a while.

Do you know...?

Flying geese and other birds can be a hazard to aircraft. Every year, birds colliding with planes cause millions of pounds worth of damage. It has even been known for geese to be sucked into a plane's engine.

How did the barnacle goose get its name?

In olden times, barnacle geese counted as fish!

Do you know...?

Barnacle geese often nest on high cliffs. When the young hatch, they have to get down quickly because there is no food for them on the cliffs. They can't fly, so they jump. Lots of them are hurt or killed on the way down or when they land.

Hundreds of years ago, in medieval times, European people believed that these geese hatched from a small, shelled sea creature called a barnacle. Barnacles live on timber and other materials that are constantly soaked in salt water. Both the geese and the barnacles, which are called goose barnacles, are coloured black and white. You can just about see that a barnacle might look like a very small goose. Because the geese were not seen in Europe in the winter, they were believed to be growing under water. Barnacle geese were often eaten, and for religious reasons were sometimes regarded as fish! By thinking of the birds in this way, Christians who were allowed to eat fish, but not meat, on Fridays, could enjoy a meal of goose.

How do herons keep their feathers in good condition ?

All birds spend hours every day preening, which means cleaning and tidying their plumage. To condition their feathers, many birds coat them with oil that they take with their beaks from a gland near their tails. Herons are just as fussy about good grooming as any other bird, but they have a different way of keeping their feathers looking good.

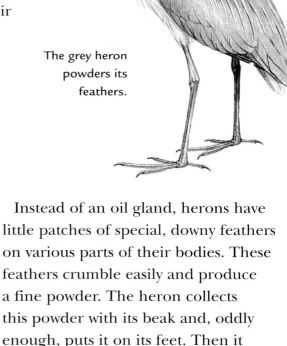

The grey heron powders its feathers.

Do you know...?

Herons are able to gulp down quite large prey, including big fish and even mammals such as rats. They can do this because their throats are very elastic and stretch when the herons swallow.

Instead of an oil gland, herons have little patches of special, downy feathers on various parts of their bodies. These feathers crumble easily and produce a fine powder. The heron collects this powder with its beak and, oddly enough, puts it on its feet. Then it uses its feet to 'comb' the powder through its feathers, which cleans and conditions them.

CHAPTER 4
HUNTERS, FISHERS & SCAVENGERS

How do vultures find the remains of dead animals?

Vultures soar high above the African savanna in search of their next meal.

Vultures are scavengers, which means they eat the remains of dead animals. Scavenging vultures have excellent vision and they are always on the lookout for their next meal. The vultures soar at great height, using this vantage point to scan over a wide area and pick out dead and dying animals on the open ground. Vultures are gregarious – they live in groups. As soon as one bird drops down to investigate a possible source of food, you can be sure that the others will rapidly follow. The vultures then jostle violently with each other as they compete for their share of the food.

Do you know...?

As well as their excellent eyesight, vultures use their keen sense of smell to find food. After a day or two, the decaying remains of a dead animal give off a foul stench. The vultures home in on the smell to find their meal.

Why do peregrines seem to like living in cities?

The swift and deadly peregrine falcon lives in many parts of the world, from the tropics to the tundra. Some can also be found in busy city centres. In the wild, the peregrine prefers to build a nest on a tall cliff or crag. In the city, it makes use of a tower or some other tall building, nesting on a narrow window ledge. There is lots of food for the urban peregrine. From its vantage point, high above the streets, these efficient killers swoop down on unsuspecting pigeons or starlings.

The peregrine is the perfect urban assassin.

Do you know...?

Peregrine falcons have few natural predators, but their eggs are vulnerable to nest robbers, such as foxes. The peregrine will usually build its nest, or scrape, high above the ground. In cities, it uses a suitably tall structure, such as a chimney, tower or bridge.

How does a vulture fly without flapping its wings?

The laws of physics apply to birds as much as they do to aeroplanes. When a bird flies, the flow of air over its wings creates a force called lift. As the bird flaps its wings, it creates an extra force called thrust. These forces overcome the bird's weight and any drag forces acting on its body. Some large birds, such as eagles and vultures, fly without flapping their wings. These birds soar through the skies, wings outstretched, for hours on end. This is possible because lift creates upwards and forwards forces on the bird's body, keeping the bird aloft as it glides through the air.

Do you know...?

Vultures and other gliding birds are very heavy. They would use up a lot of energy if they had to flap their wings to stay aloft. Instead, these birds glide on rising air currents, called thermals, which are formed as sunlight warms the Earth's surface.

A vulture soars through the sky.

Which bird builds the biggest nests?

The bald eagle builds one of the biggest nests of the bird world. The largest bald eagle nests measure about 2.5 metres across and weigh several tonnes. Weaver birds build some of the biggest colonial nests. These birds weave their amazing nests and then hang them from the branches of tall trees. The word 'colonial' means that large groups of weavers hang their nests together. Hammerkops build some of the largest and most impressive enclosed nests. The domes of these nests can stand 2 metres tall and can measure 2 metres across. The nest is so strong that a person could walk on the nest without damaging it.

The bald eagle has one of the biggest nests.

Do you know...?

The Australian megapodes do not build nests. They bury their eggs under huge mounds of soil and rotting vegetation. The size of some megapode mounds is amazing. The dusky scrubfowl builds a mound that measures about 11 metres across and stands 5 metres tall.

How have red kites been saved from extinction?

With its reddish-brown plumage and deeply forked tail, the red kite is a spectacular sight in the sky. Once common throughout Britain, these birds were hunted for sport. By the end of the 19th century, the red kite was almost extinct. Only a few birds survived in Wales. Efforts to save the species started in 1989, when red kites from Spain and Sweden were released into the wild in England and Scotland. The birds started to breed, and the population slowly recovered. Native chicks have since been re-introduced to other parts of Britain with great success.

Do you know...?

Red kites were once a common sight on the streets of cities across Britain. Indeed, William Shakespeare described London as 'the city of kites and crows' in his tragedy *Coriolanus*. Red kites were the ultimate city scavengers, eating any scraps of food left out on the street.

The population of red kites in Britain is steadily increasing.

Why do reddish egrets shade the water with their wings?

The reddish egret chases its prey.

The reddish egret, a type of heron, is a striking bird that lives near coastal marshes in the southern United States, Central America and the Caribbean. It is a keen hunter, feeding on insects, crustaceans and frogs, living around tropical swamps and tidal flats. The bird has an unusual trick to catch fish. Reddish egrets can often be seen in the water, holding their wings out like an umbrella. Called 'canopy feeding', the wings shade the water and attract the fish – easy pickings for the hungry egret.

Do you know...?

Herons use a range of techniques to trap prey. These skilled hunters can be very patient. Some herons will stand perfectly still in the water, waiting to spear any passing fish. Others actively disturb their prey, stirring up the muddy riverbed with their feet to flush out a tasty snack.

Huge, forward-facing eyes help the eagle strike with accuracy.

Just how good is an eagle's eyesight?

Compared to our own eyesight, an eagle can see in amazing detail. These birds use their excellent vision to look for food. An eagle can pick out the outline of a mouse from a distance of 3 kilometres or more. Some eagles can also see under water up to a depth of around 10 metres, picking out fish as they swim up to the surface of the water. The eagle's excellent vision is due to its enormous eyes. Each eyeball takes up around one quarter of the space of the skull. There's little room for anything else!

Do you know...?

In addition to the size of its eyes, the eagle's vision is helped by the presence of cone cells. The cones help the eagle to pick out colour in greater detail, but this also makes seeing in the dark much more difficult. Eagles also have stereo vision. This means that they can see both forwards and sideways at the same time, providing greater all-round vision.

How do peregrines reach such great speeds in flight?

No other animal on the planet can match the peregrine falcon's swoop for sheer speed. Agile and accurate, the peregrine uses its swoop to devastating effect when hunting. These deadly birds circle high in the sky, looking for a suitable victim, such as a starling. Once the prey has been pinpointed, the drama unfolds in seconds.

The peregrine's sheer speed is too much for a passing pigeon or a starling.

Do you know...?

Diving at a speed of almost 100 metres per second, the peregrine falcon is the fastest animal on Earth.

Moving quickly, the peregrine tips head first into its astonishing dive. The bird drops vertically through the sky, picking up speed as it closes its wings slightly to reduce the drag over its body. Moving at up to 360 km/h, the peregrine has usually killed its unfortunate victim outright by the time its outstretched talons strike its target. In some cases, however, the peregrine's attack fails at the first attempt. The bird then simply swoops round and bursts into sustained, level flight in order to overcome its prey.

How does an osprey hang on to slippery fish?

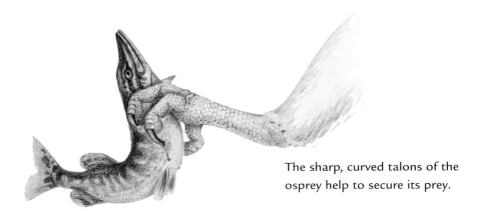

The sharp, curved talons of the osprey help to secure its prey.

Over millions of years, the osprey has developed a unique combination of characteristics that make it one of the most successful of all the fishing birds of prey. For a start, an osprey's feathers are water resistant. Submerged, the osprey can close its nostrils to stop water from leaking into its lungs. The osprey then extends its long, curved talons deep into the water to skewer its prey. Sharp, spiny scales on the soles of the osprey's feet help the bird retain a grip on its slippery victim as it is carried back to the feeding perch.

Do you know...?

The sharp talons and spiny scales on the osprey's feet are so effective at gripping a slippery fish, that sometimes the bird becomes laden down with a fish that is heavier than expected. The extra weight may drag the osprey back into the water, and it is not unheard of for an osprey to drown in this way.

How do pesticides affect birds of prey?

There is an established link between the use of certain pesticides and the decline in birds such as eagles and other birds of prey. Originally designed to kill pests that eat our crops, such as rats and mice, organochlorine pesticides can build up inside the pests' bodies without killing them. In turn, the infected rodents fall prey to birds, such as peregrine falcons and eagles. When the birds of prey eat these pests, the chemicals pass directly into their own bodies. Some pesticides, such as DDT, damage the eggs of the adults so they cannot produce offspring. Stronger pesticides, such as dieldrin, kill the birds outright. Organochlorine pesticides have now been banned in North America and Europe, but are used in other parts of the world.

Do you know...?

Farmers began using DDT on crops in the 1940s. A highly effective pesticide, it slowly built up in animals higher up the food chain, including humans. As a result, most countries had banned DDT by the late 1980s.

Ospreys are on the up in Europe and the USA.

Why do vultures have bald heads?

Vultures feed on a rotting carcass.

Do you know...?

The bald eagle's name is slightly misleading. This bird isn't bald at all; the head is covered with striking, white feathers, as is the tail, while the body is brown. Only the adults have the white head that gives the species its name.

For vultures, it's good to be bald. These birds are scavengers and feed on the remains of dead animals. When they eat, vultures like to thrust their heads deep inside a carcass, tearing off scraps of soft flesh with their sharp, hooked beaks. But none of the bloody bits stick to the bird, since the head and neck lack feathers. Having a bare, featherless head also reduces the chance of infection when these birds feed on half-rotten meat.

Why don't eagles stop their chicks from bullying each other?

Most female eagles lay two eggs, but only one chick will usually survive to become an adult. The first chick to hatch will bully its younger brother or sister and take nearly all the food brought to the nest by its parents. Eventually, malnourished and weak, the younger chick dies and will be thrown from the nest without mercy. This may sound horrible to people, but eagles don't share human emotions. The parents allow the bullying strategy, because it ensures that only the stronger chicks survive.

Do you know...?

Eagles invest a lot of time in caring for their young. Both parents take an active role: dad typically provides the food, while mum feeds and tends the nestlings. As the chicks grow, both parents need to hunt in order to satisfy the appetite of their hungry offspring.

A pair of eagle eggs in a nest.

Why is the bald eagle the symbol of the USA?

The origin of the bald eagle as a national symbol of the USA dates back to 20 June 1782. On that day, the Continental Congress, the first American government, officially adopted the current design for the Great Seal of the United States. The seal features a bald eagle, wings outstretched, clutching an olive branch in its right talon and

The bald eagle is a proud symbol of America, found on national seals and several coins.

Do you know...?

Benjamin Franklin didn't support the use of the bald eagle as a symbol of the USA. He described the bald eagle as 'a rank coward' and favoured using the turkey, calling it 'a bird of courage'.

13 arrows in its left talon. The arrows represent the original 13 states, and the olive branch is a symbol of peace. The founding fathers of the USA chose the bald eagle because the bird is unique to North America. The image of this magnificent bird has come to represent America's spirit, freedom and pursuit of excellence. The bald eagle is also a sacred bird among Native American tribes. They use the bird's feathers in many religious and spiritual customs.

Why do owls have such good night vision?

The most noticeable feature of an owl is the bird's wide, staring eyes.

Do you know...?

An owl has binocular vision, which means it can see in three dimensions. This is essential for a hunter that needs to judge distance accurately. People also see in three dimensions – our ancestors lived in trees and judging distance was also vital.

Most owls prefer to hunt at night. They emerge at dusk, sweeping through the air on silent wings. An owl's eyes are specially adapted to help it to see at night. The owl uses them to gather as much light as possible. Tiny cells inside the eye, called rods, work well in low light but cannot process colour. So the owl sees in great detail at night, but the images only appear in black and white.

Why do small birds mob birds of prey?

Mobbing is a noisy display that some birds use as a form of defence against predators such as birds of prey. When threatened, the brave birds fly at the bird of prey, emitting loud alarm calls to distract and harass the predator. Sometimes the birds will risk making physical contact with the predator to drive it away. The display starts off with one or two small birds, but the noise and commotion often attracts many others to the scene. Sometimes, different species join in to drive away the threat. Since there is safety in numbers, even very small birds, such as tits, can successfully drive away a bird of prey.

Do you know...?

The mobbing calls of different birds share certain characteristics. The calls are loud and sharp, and they usually start and end suddenly. In this way, birds can recognise the calls of different species.

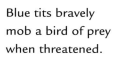

Blue tits bravely mob a bird of prey when threatened.

Why do shrikes impale their prey on thorns?

Shrikes are attractive and colourful songbirds, but they are also deadly hunters. They are famous for impaling their prey on sharp thorns. There are two reasons for this rather gruesome behaviour. When feeding, the thorns help secure the prey while the shrike rips it into bite-sized pieces. But the shrike also leaves many of its impaled victims as a store of food. This unusual behaviour has earned the shrike its alternative name – the butcher bird.

The great grey shrike impales its next victim on a sharp thorn.

Do you know...?

Some insects produce foul chemicals as a defence against predators. But the effects of the chemicals are often short-lived. The shrike's grisly habit of skewering its prey as a food store means the chemicals break down. The insect prey is then safe to eat.

Vultures look prehistoric – how old are they really?

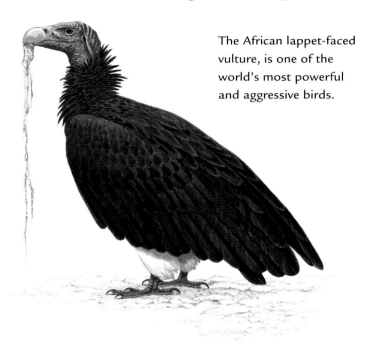

The African lappet-faced vulture, is one of the world's most powerful and aggressive birds.

Fossils have shown that the first vulture-like birds appeared on the Earth no earlier than 25 million years ago. In fact, two very different vulture groups evolved from completely different ancestors. Species belonging to the two groups look very similar, share many characteristics and even share the name 'vulture', but they are not related. Old World vultures, such as the griffon and the lammergeyer, live in Africa and Asia and share ancestors with eagles and hawks. New World vultures, such as the Andean condor and the turkey vulture, are found in North and South America and are closely related to storks.

Do you know...?

The most likely contender for the earliest bird is *Archaeopteryx*, which was alive when dinosaurs roamed the Earth, about 150 million years ago.

Which is the smallest bird of prey?

The African pygmy falcon is one of the world's smallest birds of prey.

The tiny falconets, such as the white-fronted falconet of Borneo and the black-legged falconet of South-east Asia, typically weigh about 35 grams and measure around 15 centimetres from head to tail. This would make them the world's smallest birds of prey. African pygmy falcons, however, are generally about the same size, although some do weigh as much as 50 grams and can measure up to 19 centimetres from head to tail.

Do you know...?

African pygmy falcons and Asian falconets are rarely bigger than a common starling (right). They feed mainly on large insects and lizards. Occasionally they hunt small birds, which they catch in the air, in much the same way as their larger falcon relatives do.

How do kingfishers hunt?

A malachite kingfisher with a freshly caught fish.

The kingfisher is a skilled hunter. This attractive bird hunts for sticklebacks and other small fish. When fishing, the kingfisher rests on a perch by the water's edge. It uses its sharp eyesight to watch for fish darting just below the surface. When the bird spots a meal, it dives head first into the water. The kingfisher then grabs the unfortunate fish in its beak, emerges from the water and returns to its perch. Having killed the fish by bashing it against the perch, the kingfisher then swallows its meal head first.

Do you know...?

The kingfisher is a fussy eater. It prefers to kill its victim before swallowing it. In this way the scales do not get stuck in the bird's throat. The kingfisher can digest the meat, but the bones and scales are thrown back up as a small pellet.

Which is the highest-flying bird?

The highest-flying bird ever recorded is a type of vulture called a Ruppell's griffon. On 29 November 1975, the bird was sucked into the jet engine of an aeroplane flying more than 11,500 metres above the Ivory Coast in Africa. You would have to climb another 2 kilometres above the summit of Mount Everest to reach that height! The bird obviously died, but the pilot managed to land the damaged aircraft safely. Ruppell's griffon is not the only high-flyer. Other birds regularly brave high altitudes during their seasonal migrations. The bar-headed goose migrates from India to Tibet, for example, flying over the Himalayas to get there.

Ruppell's griffon takes the prize for being the highest-flying bird.

Do you know...?

The air is very thin at high altitude, but most birds can still breathe. A bird's breathing system is unique. The air circulates through a bird's lungs twice for every single breath, before being exhaled. This increases the oxygen intake, making it easier to breathe.

Which is the largest animal hunted by a bird of prey?

The howl, or roar, of the slow-moving howler monkey can be heard from as far away as 5 kilometres.

Do you know...?

Only the female harpy eagles tend to hunt large prey such as howlers. Like most eagles, the females are almost twice the size of the males. The males prefer to hunt smaller prey such as opossums, porcupines and reptiles.

With a wingspan of more than 2 metres and talons longer and sharper than a bear's claws, the harpy eagle is a fearsome predator. This large, powerful eagle lives in the rainforests of Central and South America. The black howler is one of the largest monkeys in the Americas. It also lives in the rainforest, where it feeds on flowers, fruits and leaves at the top of the rainforest canopy. A hungry harpy eagle can easily pick off one of these slow-moving monkeys, so the howlers have to be constantly on the lookout for an aerial attack.

Why are there so many folk stories about storks?

The white stork is the subject of many folk stories.

S een as a symbol of good fortune and happiness, history is littered with stories about white storks. One of the most common myths was born in Victorian Britain. The Victorians did not like talking about sex, so they made up a story about a

Do you know...?

The stork has a strong attachment to its nest, and this is another reason for stork myths. So it is considered to be very lucky if a stork builds its nest on the roof of your house. And it is considered to be very unlucky if the stork then abandons its nest.

white stork delivering a newborn baby wrapped in a sling. In many folk stories, the stork is also seen as a symbol of devotion and loyalty, thanks to the bird's supposed habit of mating with just one partner. In fact, the bond lasts for only one season.

How does a kestrel hover?

The kestrel hovers more than any other bird of prey.

The kestrel is a truly agile hunter. These small falcons can often be seen hovering above a grassy verge, hanging in the air as they scan the ground for small rodents, such as voles. But it takes a great deal of effort and agility to stay in one spot. The kestrel beats its wings six times a second, moving its tail like a rudder as the wind buffets the bird's body. All this time, the kestrel keeps its head perfectly still, so it can pick out any tiny movements on the ground. The kestrel then swoops down to the ground to pounce on its prey.

Do you know...?

Hovering takes up much more energy than hunting from a perch. But kestrels catch more food on the wing. Kestrels hover more in the summer than in the winter. This is because, in summer, the kestrel usually has many more mouths to feed.

How are California condors hand-reared?

The California condor was on the brink of extinction but now looks set to recover.

The California condor is one of the rarest birds in the world. By 1987, the population was so low that the American government decided to capture the last few wild condors and keep them in captivity. When the captive condors started to breed and produce chicks, the zoologists helped them to rear their young. The female condor lays a single egg in two clutches. So the zoologists took the first egg and reared it using a puppet shaped like an adult condor. The condors were then left to rear the second egg.

Do you know...?

The condor captive-breeding programme was so successful that zoologists started to release condors back into the wild in 1991. The population of wild condors has steadily grown, as more captive-bred condors have been released and have started to breed in the wild.

Which is the world's biggest bird of prey?

In terms of sheer size, the biggest bird of prey is the Eurasian black vulture. This giant of the skies may stretch to over a metre in length, with a wingspan of 3 metres. Up to 12.5 kilograms in weight, these vultures are also some of the heaviest flying birds. The Eurasian black vulture also goes by the names monk vulture and cinereous vulture. Although it shares a similar name and colour, the Eurasian black vulture is unrelated to the American black vulture. The number of Eurasian black vultures has steadily dropped in the last 200 years, particularly in western Europe.

The enormous black vulture lives throughout Europe and Asia.

Do you know...?

The European eagle owl is the world's biggest owl in terms of weight and overall length. But opinion is divided, since the great grey owl can also be quite long. The fluffy plumage of the great grey owl, however, adds more to its bulk than to its physical size.

How can an owl twist its head so far round?

An owl cannot move its eyes to look around. Instead, the bird moves its entire head. The owl has excellent eyesight. Since the eyes are big, they are very good at gathering light. But the eyes are so big that the owl cannot roll or move its eyes – owls can only look straight ahead. Instead, the owl's neck can stretch so the head can turn through an amazing degree of rotation. Indeed, the owl can turn its head almost completely around and upside down to look in any direction.

The barn owl's flexible neck allows it to turn its head in any direction.

Do you know...?

It is not only the owl's vision that is so acute. These birds can hear with an amazing degree of accuracy. The faces of some owls are shaped like discs. These 'facial discs' act like mini radar dishes, guiding even the slightest movement made by approaching prey to the bird's ears.

How do condors soar so well?

The Andean condor soars over the rugged Andes Mountains in search of food.

Do you know...?

When a condor flies, you can see gaps at the ends of the outstretched wings. These so-called wing slots let the condor make minor adjustments to its flight path, much like the wing flaps that are on an aeroplane.

Close up it may not look the most attractive bird, but there are few sights as graceful as a condor soaring through the sky. Andean condors are high-flyers, soaring to heights of more than 5,500 metres. These birds are born to glide. The vast wingspan of up to 3 metres provides a huge lifting force as air passes over the wings. The condor is one of the heaviest flying birds – too heavy to fly without assistance. So it looks for updrafts of warm air, known as thermals, to keep airborne. It saves energy by gliding between thermals, flapping its wings about once every hour.

How fast can a roadrunner run?

Made famous by the Warner Bros. cartoon character, Wile E. Coyote, 'roadrunner' is the name given to two different birds – the greater roadrunner and the lesser roadrunner. Both of these birds make their homes in the scrublands and deserts of the south-western United States and Mexico. Roadrunners are able to fly, but they spend most of their time on the ground, hunting down their prey, which include insects, scorpions and spiders, small reptiles, rodents and other small mammals. When the roadrunner is in pursuit of its prey, it frequently travels at speeds of up to 25 km/h.

Do you know...?

In the 1940s cartoon, Wile E. Coyote is usually silent and the roadrunner makes only one sound – 'beep beep'. Roadrunners, in fact, make a very slow, descending, cooing sound in the wild. It is very much like the cooing of a dove.

The greater roadrunner sprints after a range of prey, including snakes and small lizards.

What is in an owl pellet?

Owls get rid of the food they cannot digest in the form of small pellets. A pellet contains material such as animal bones, claws and beaks, which are too tough and hard to be broken down by the owl's digestive juices. Once the owl has eaten its prey, the food passes into a chamber called the gizzard. There, the food is broken up ready for digestion in the stomach. However, the hard parts of the prey's body remain in the gizzard. The gizzard squeezes this material into a pellet, which then passes out of the bird's mouth. Most owls cough up two or three of these pellets every day.

Do you know...?

Owls provide zoologists with information about small mammals, which are easy to identify using the skulls and bones found in the pellets. These studies further our understanding about food chains and the role of the owl in them.

The great horned owl hunts small mammals and birds, but it will also feed on the remains of dead animals.

What is falconry?

Falconry is the rearing and training of birds of prey to hunt game animals. In the past, this centuries-old sport was seen as the preserve of the rich and noble classes. Today, however, people from many, very different backgrounds are involved in falconry. The most popular birds used in the sport are the red-tailed hawk and Harris's hawk. These birds are especially good for beginners to handle. More experienced falconers usually move on to goshawks, peregrines, owls and even the large eagles. In most countries, only captive-bred birds can be used. Often, this has led to the recovery of several endangered species.

Beginners to the sport of falconry often start with a small bird, such as a kestrel.

Do you know...?

There is a very long list of famous falconers, thanks to the sport's noble associations. Indeed, many kings and queens were involved in falconry up until the 19th century. Most employed a falconer to rear and train the birds, as this historic French statue shows.

How does a barn owl fly so silently?

Barn owls need to fly very quietly so they can listen out for the tiny movements made by prey such as rodents. By flying so silently, the barn owl is also unlikely to alert the prey and scare it away. To help them fly without making a noise, the barn owl has very soft feathers.

Do you know...?

A barn owl's feathers may be soft, but they are not very waterproof. So these owls do not like hunting in wet weather. Barn owls have also been known to drown in water troughs when taking a drink.

The barn owl's soft feathers help it to fly almost completely silently.

The front edges of the owl's wing feathers also have soft edges to muffle the sound it makes when the bird flaps its wings. Like most birds, baby owls are covered with light yet warm feathers called down. The young owls gradually shed the down feathers, and the special adult feathers then grow in their place.

CHAPTER 5
PLANT LOVERS

Why do hornbills seal themselves in their nesting holes?

For about four months the female hornbill stays walled up in her nest hole in a tree. She chooses her nest site and partly seals the entrance from the outside with mud. Then she moves in and works from the inside until just a narrow opening remains. The hornbill uses her own droppings as cement! Hornbills probably seal their nests to prevent rival birds from taking over the hole and to keep out predators, such as snakes. The male feeds the female and her new chicks through the gap. Later, the female breaks out through the hole to help with the feeding. The chicks seal up the door again all by themselves. They emerge when it's time to learn to fly.

Hornbills seal up their nest holes to make them secure.

Do you know...?

When a female hornbill is nesting, she moults her tail feathers and the big flight feathers on her wings. While the hornbill is in the nest, the feathers regrow. By the time the female emerges, her new feathers are all in place.

124

Why did the dodo become extinct?

This is what the dodo might have looked like.

No one has seen a living dodo for well over 300 years. This large, flightless bird used to live on the island of Mauritius in the Indian Ocean. It thrived there until European people began to visit the island at the beginning of the 16th century. Dodos were clumsy birds and easy to catch, so sailors used to trap them for food. Later, when Europeans actually settled on Mauritius, they brought cats and dogs, which preyed on dodo eggs and chicks. By the end of the 17th century, the dodo was extinct. Present-day scientists only know what the dodo looked like from the descriptions and drawings of sailors. However, these descriptions may not have been accurate. A few fossil remains were also found on Mauritius, which helped to build up a picture of the dodo.

Do you know...?

The dodo was related to the pigeon – but it was a very big pigeon! It is estimated that an adult dodo must have weighed over 20 kilograms. Its tiny wings could not have lifted such a large bird off the ground.

How do parrots open nuts and seeds?

A parrot's hooked beak makes short work of hard nutshells.

Do you know...?

A parrot has two toes pointing forwards and two pointing backwards. These toes give a parrot an extremely powerful grip for perching. They can also be used like hands to pick things up.

Parrots have beaks that are perfect for cracking open hard nutshells and the husks of seeds. The upper half, or mandible, of a parrot's beak is large and curves downwards. It fits closely over the shorter, lower mandible. The upper mandible is attached to the bird's skull with a flexible hinge and can be moved easily. A parrot feeds by gripping a seed between the sharp tip of the lower mandible and the ridged edge of the upper mandible. Then the parrot twirls the seed rapidly round and round with its tongue until the sharp beak splits the husk. The bird drops the husk and swallows the seed.

Why is a trumpeter's social life unusual?

A trumpeter stays with its flock all year round.

Family and friends are important to trumpeters. These noisy South American forest birds do everything in sociable groups. They live mostly on the ground and move around in flocks that may contain up to 20 birds. One bird sets itself up as head of a flock and leads its troops around their territory to feed. Trumpeters don't put up with trespassers. If the home flock hears strangers, they all rush together to send the intruders packing. The trumpeters make threatening moves with their heads and lowered wings. Any trespassers that fail to make a run for it risk being severely pecked and kicked. Only one female in a flock of trumpeters has chicks. The whole group shares in their care and protection.

Do you know...?

Trumpeters perform rituals when they wake from roosting to strengthen the bonds of the flock. Less important birds crouch in front of the more important birds, making begging calls like hungry chicks. This is a way of saying that they know their place!

How many different types of parrot are there?

Do you know...?

Tame parrots are much loved for their amusing imitations of the human voice. Bird researchers have had some success in teaching parrots to use the correct words to name objects or to ask for something.

There are over 350 species, or different types, of parrot. Many are brightly coloured, while others are white, grey or black. Macaws from Central and South America are the most spectacular parrots, with long tails and vividly coloured plumage. Australian cockatoos often have showy crests of feathers on their heads. The biggest parrot is the flightless kakapo, which can weigh up to 3 kilograms. At the other extreme are pygmy parrots, which tip the scales at around 10 grams.

Parrots come in all sizes and colours.

How do toucans eat fruit?

When a toucan feeds on fruits, such as small berries, it uses just the tip of its beak to twist or pull a juicy item off a branch. But it's a long way from the tip of this massive beak to the back of the toucan's throat. The toucan has a smart way of getting over this problem. Holding the fruit lightly, the bird tosses it high in the air. At the same time, the toucan opens its beak wide. The fruit lands in the bird's throat and is instantly swallowed whole. Toucans never seem to miss their aim! To eat bigger fruits with tough skins, toucans break up the food with their beaks to get at the insides.

A toucan's diet contains a lot of fruit.

Do you know...?

Soft, squishy fruit makes beaks sticky, so toucans always clean themselves up after eating. They can often be seen rubbing their beaks against branches or using their feet to scrape away the remains of a meal.

Why do jays bury acorns?

Every autumn, when acorns are ripe on the oak trees, jays get very busy indeed. Day after day, they fly off to find and collect acorns. A jay packs about half a dozen acorns in its crop, a special storage pouch that birds have inside their bodies. The jay usually carries an extra acorn in its beak. After hurrying back to its home, the jay then buries the acorns in the ground and rakes fallen leaves over the top. This food is the jay's winter store. During the cold months, the bird will probably eat little else. It is believed that a jay buries about 5000 acorns every year. The birds remember where they have buried their acorns by taking note of nearby trees and other landmarks.

The American blue jay, like its European cousins, stores acorns every autumn.

Do you know...?

Many of the acorns buried by jays are not recovered. They stay in the ground and some may grow into seedling trees. This is how, over centuries, oak woods are able to spread.

How do homing pigeons navigate?

Pigeons don't get lost very easily.

Pigeons that are set free a long way from home often find a fast and accurate route back. If a pigeon is not too far from home, it steers by familiar landmarks. It may also follow smells. From further away, a pigeon might navigate by the position of the Sun. Scientists also think it is possible that the birds can navigate by using the Earth's magnetic field. In other words, pigeons probably have a built-in 'compass' that responds to natural magnetic forces.

Do you know...?

Throughout history, people have made good use of pigeons' homing instincts. For centuries, the birds were highly valued as messengers. During World War II, many pigeons were used to carry messages of vital importance during battles.

How do lorikeets eat pollen and nectar?

For a lorikeet, it's flowers for breakfast, flowers for lunch and flowers for supper. These parrots eat nothing but nectar and pollen. They have a tongue that is specially designed for getting at the sweet stuff, as well as a purpose-made digestive system.

Do you know...?

Lorikeets feed quickly and may visit as many as 5,000 flowers in one day. The pollen and nectar are very nutritious. Two meals a day are enough for a lorikeet.

A lorikeet collects nectar from many different plants.

A lorikeet takes a whole flower into its beak and slurps it around with its long tongue. At the tip of the tongue is a hair-like tuft. This collects the nectar and rolls pollen grains into balls that the bird can swallow. The lorikeets' flowery food is easy to digest. Lorikeets don't have muscly intestines like other parrots, who have to digest tough plant food. A lorikeet has weak stomach muscles and a short gut.

Why are there so many red-billed queleas?

Red-billed queleas can be counted in millions. They collect in bigger colonies than almost any other type of bird. Queleas are so numerous because they have one of the largest supplies of birdseed in the world. They live on the vast African plains, where seed-producing grasses extend as far as the eye can see. Different grass seeds ripen at different times of the year. The queleas move from area to area and season to season, following the food trail. Another reason why there are so many queleas is that the birds are very fast breeders. They take a couple of days to build a nest. Two weeks later, the chicks have hatched. In another two weeks, the young can leave the nest and fly.

Do you know...?

Flocks of red-billed queleas are bad news for farmers who grow seed-producing plants. These birds can rapidly devour a whole crop. Queleas are such pests on agricultural land that they are called 'locust birds', after the plant-destroying insects.

African farmers try to keep red-billed queleas away from their crops.

Why do macaws eat clay?

Macaws love eating clay.

Scientists think that eating clay helps macaws to avoid digestive problems. The fruits that form the main part of a macaw's diet often contain poisonous substances that would make many birds and mammals ill. It is likely that the clay soaks up the poison, leaving the good parts of the fruit to be digested. There may also be some nutrients in the clay. Macaws find their clay on high cliffs alongside riverbanks. They gather in large flocks to dig out the clay with their beaks.

Do you know...?

Feeding at the clay cliffs is one of the few reasons for macaws to leave their lofty tree tops. All the fruit they need is on the trees. Macaws don't even come down to drink that often, as they get plenty of water from their food.

Which birds have the fastest wingbeats?

Hummingbirds move their wings faster than any other type of bird. Two hundred wingbeats a second really doesn't sound possible, but the ruby-throated hummingbird can do just that! The bird

Do you know...?

Hummingbird wings have especially strong muscles. The wings are attached to the bird's body in a way that allows them to move freely in all directions. A humming bird moves its wings in a figure-of-eight pattern when hovering.

produces this phenomenal wing speed when it performs its courtship flight. And many other types of hummingbird can produce around 75 wingbeats a second, which is still pretty impressive. Hummingbirds use this amazing technique to hover in mid-air, which they do all the time as they feed on the nectar from flowers.

Super-fast wingbeats are what keep a hummingbird suspended in mid-air.

What are Darwin's finches?

These finches all had
the same ancestors.

Do you know...?

Today, Darwin's finches
face a serious threat. The
maggots of flies that feed
on the blood of finch
chicks were accidently
brought to the islands on
a ship. If the flies become
more widespread, they
may kill off the finches.

In 1835, the naturalist Charles
Darwin was on the Galapágos
Islands in the Pacific Ocean. He
observed some finches, which
seemed to be of all different types.
They had fat beaks or thin beaks or
even parrot-like beaks. Some finches
ate seeds and others lived on nectar.
Darwin's theory was that all these
finches had the same ancestors.
Over millions of years, the ancestors
had evolved into birds with different
beaks and habits to match the sort
of food that was available. Darwin's
finches are famous for helping him
to work out his theory of evolution.

Why does the sword-billed hummingbird have such a long beak?

Some beak!

The sword-billed hummingbird's beak is only about 9 centimetres long. But if you have a body that is also 9 centimetres long – just like the sword-bill – that's a terrific beak! It is, however, the perfect length for the bird to reach the food it likes. The sword-bill feeds on nectar from flowers with long, tubelike heads. The nectar, which lies at the bottom of the flowerheads, would be unreachable by a hummingbird with a shorter beak. So the sword-bill has a food supply all to itself. The bird also does the plants a favour. As it goes from flower to flower, it carries pollen from one plant to another. This fertilises the plants, enabling them to reproduce.

Do you know...?

Different types, or species, of hummingbird have beaks specially designed for feeding on particular flowers. Some have long, thin beaks that fit perfectly into narrow flowers. Others have curvy beaks, that are just right for dipping into curved flowerheads. Some hummingbirds have short, strong beaks that are used to pierce holes in flowers.

What do hummingbirds' nests look like?

Do you know...?

Using spiders' webs not only makes a hummingbird's nest strong, it makes it stretchy as well! The web is very elastic and allows the nest to expand as the hummingbird chicks grow bigger.

Nest-building is the responsibility of the female hummingbird, and she makes a beautiful job of it. She carefully chooses a safe, sheltered place in a tree or a bush. In the case of the giant hummingbird, the ideal spot may be on top of a cactus. Then the hummingbird begins the task of weaving her nest from a mixture of grasses, leaves and other plant fibres. Some hummingbird nests are shaped like tiny cups, while others are like a hanging pouch. The female lines her nest with something soft, such as feathers. To make their nests stronger, hummingbirds sometimes use spiders' webs to bind the plant fibres together. They may also put patches of moss or lichen on the outside, which look like miniature tiles.

A black-chinned hummingbird sits in her cup-like nest.

How do Pallas's sandgrouse give their chicks water?

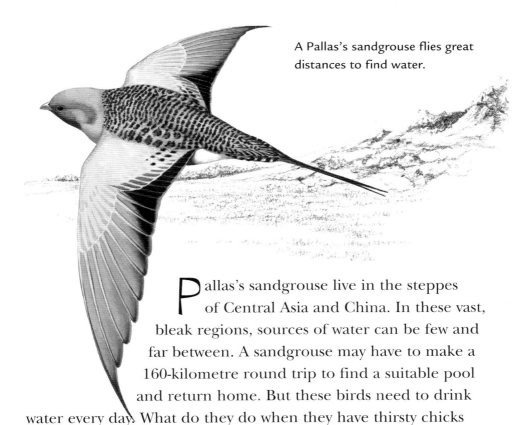

A Pallas's sandgrouse flies great distances to find water.

Pallas's sandgrouse live in the steppes of Central Asia and China. In these vast, bleak regions, sources of water can be few and far between. A sandgrouse may have to make a 160-kilometre round trip to find a suitable pool and return home. But these birds need to drink water every day. What do they do when they have thirsty chicks that cannot fly? The male sandgrouse makes sure that his brood get enough to drink. He has special feathers on his belly designed to soak up a lot of water. When he visits a drinking pool, he makes himself soaking wet. On his return to the nest, the chicks gather round to take water from his feathers.

Do you know...?

There are many types of sandgrouse and they all live in dry regions with few sources of water. They drink once a day, always at the same time. Sometimes flocks of more than a thousands birds gather at one pool.

Why are macaws threatened?

Macaws cannot survive without tall trees, which provide them with food and safe places to nest. If the trees are under threat, then so are the macaws. Sadly, this is exactly what is happening in the forests of Central and South America, where macaws live. People are destroying the trees to clear the forests for settlements and farmland, and to build roads and mines. The macaw is at risk from people in other ways, too. These birds are often trapped, illegally, to be sold as cagebirds. Worse still, macaws are sometimes hunted and killed simply because people want to take their magnificent feathers. Conservationists are trying hard to protect macaws and their forests. But in some regions the birds have already vanished.

Do you know...?

A few years ago, the rare Spix's macaw of Brazil became extinct in the wild. Just one last bird had been clinging on to survival, and then it disappeared. A small number of Spix's macaws live in captivity.

When forest trees disappear, so do macaws.

Which is the world's smallest bird?

The bee hummingbird is the tiniest bird in the world.

Birds don't get any smaller than the bee hummingbird, which is found in Cuba. This tiny scrap of feathers is barely 6 centimetres long from beak to tail and weighs less than 2 grams. And there are plenty of other hummingbirds almost as small. In fact, even the biggest of them, the giant hummingbird, is hardly a heavyweight at around 20 grams. For their size, hummingbirds are amazingly strong and energetic. They put more effort into their flying than any other bird in the world. And they spend many more hours a day on the go than most birds. Being so little and quick means that hummingbirds usually manage to avoid any predators.

Do you know...?

Tiny birds lose their body heat very quickly. To make energy to create heat, they feed constantly during the day. They can't store much energy to last them through the night, so they have an energy-saving device. Their heart rate and breathing slow right down while they are asleep.

This bee is about half the size of the bee hummingbird.

141

Where do budgerigars come from?

These small parrots are kept as enchanting pets nearly all over the world. But if you went to Australia, you would see more budgerigars than you thought possible. They wouldn't be in cages, however, but flying free in large flocks. Australia is the budgerigars' native land. Here, they live wild in a variety of habitats, from woods and farmland to desert areas. They feed on grass seeds and make their nests in tree holes. Wild budgerigars travel from place to place, looking for feeding sites. Because the Australian climate can be very dry, the budgerigars have to go wherever enough rain falls to make grasses grow. Where there is a good source of food, hundreds of thousands of budgerigars can often been seen gathered together.

Do you know...?

Budgerigars are easily tamed and are soon happy to perch on a finger or fly round a room. They can be taught to talk and rapidly learn a lot of words. Cared for properly, budgerigars breed well in captivity.

Budgerigars get on well with people.

Which birds build bowers?

This type of bowerbird lives in New Guinea.

Bowerbirds build bowers! A bower is an elaborate construction made of materials, such as twigs and grass and is often decked out with ornaments. Bowerbirds are from Australia and New Guinea. Only the males make bowers, which are designed to attract females. Some bowers look like little huts, others resemble patterned rugs or an 'avenue' between two walls. Bowerbirds like to decorate their structures with bright feathers, leaves and fruit. They also add any bits of coloured glass or plastic that take their fancy. Male bowerbirds sit in their bowers and sing. If a female turns up, the male starts to dance and show off in order to lure her into the bower.

Do you know...?

Some bowerbirds actually decorate their bowers with paint. They use a mixture of charcoal and saliva, which they paint on with a 'brush' of plant fibre held in their beaks.

What is being done to stop the salmon-crested cockatoo from becoming extinct in the wild?

Also known as the Moluccan cockatoo, this beautiful parrot comes from Indonesia. It is very popular as a pet. Unfortunately, this popularity led to salmon-crested cockatoos being captured from the wild in their thousands and sold for the cagebird trade. Although many of them live in captivity, these cockatoos have become extremely rare in the wild. Trapping cockatoos is now illegal and, since the late 1980s, there has been a ban on their export from Indonesia. Several programmes to encourage local people to protect the cockatoo have also been set up.

Do you know...?

Salmon-crested cockatoos make very loyal and affectionate pets, but they can also be very difficult to handle. Sadly, some end up in rescue centres, abandoned by owners who could not cope with their wayward habits.

This cockatoo faces extinction in the wild.

Why do birds of paradise have such spectacular plumage?

Male birds of paradise use their fantastic feathers to attract females – and no wonder the girls are impressed. The males usually have richly coloured body feathers, sometimes with lacy plumes. And as for their tails! There are tails with curls and whirls, tails of trailing wires, and tails in elaborate coils. When birds of paradise display their finery, they dance and spread their wings, or bounce around, plumes waving. They even swing upside down from branches, uttering loud calls.

Lacy feathers and long tail wires adorn the blue bird of paradise.

Do you know...?

Once birds of paradise have mated, the show is over as far as the males are concerned. They leave the females to make nests, sit on their eggs and feed the chicks entirely on their own.

How does a hornbill use its huge beak?

Few birds have such a massive beak as the hornbill. In many species, or types, of hornbill, the beak is topped by a horn-like structure called a casque. Despite its size, the hornbill's beak isn't very heavy. But it is powerful enough for crushing small birds and mammals to death before the hornbill eats them.

Hornbills look top heavy, but their beaks don't weigh very much.

Do you know...?

The beaks and part of the plumage of some hornbills are stained a deep yellow colour. This colour comes from a yellow oil that the bird takes from a gland near its tail and uses for preening its feathers.

The edges of the hornbill's beak are ridged, so that the bird can easily cut through tough fruit skins to get at the soft pulp inside. Yet a hornbill can also use its beak so gently that it can pluck a tiny berry from a tree without squashing it. Holding the prize at the very tip of its beak, the hornbill flips the berry, with bull's-eye accuracy, right down into its mouth.

Why were resplendent quetzals protected by the Aztecs and the Maya?

In the days of the ancient Aztec and Mayan people of Mexico and Central America, anyone who killed a resplendent quetzal was sentenced to death. The birds were regarded as sacred. The male quetzal has brilliant green and red plumage and streaming tail feathers. A quetzal's tail can grow up to 65 centimetres long. The Aztecs and the Maya used the tail feathers to make headdresses for royalty and high priests. They trapped the quetzals, took the feathers and then released the birds, otherwise unharmed, to re-grow their tails.

The resplendent quetzal's tail can grow to twice the length of its body.

Do you know...?

After the Aztec and Mayan civilisations had disappeared, the resplendent quetzal was no longer protected as a sacred bird. Over the centuries, many were killed. Today, quetzals are faced with the destruction of their forest homes.

147

Why are malachite sunbirds so fierce?

These small tropical birds are delicate-looking, with their long dainty beaks. The males have gorgeous, metallic-green feathers that gleam different colours in the sun. For its size, the male sunbird is astonishingly ferocious. All birds are quick to defend their territories, especially in the breeding season, but this sunbird is more than ready to attack all year round. It won't stand for any other bird coming near its feeding or nesting places. Whether it is another sunbird or something much larger, the malachite sunbird deals with them all in the same aggressive manner. He drives off the unwanted visitors and gives chase over huge distances. If the sunbird does catch up with an intruder he is likely to knock the fleeing bird to the ground.

The malachite sunbird shows no mercy to intruders.

Do you know...?

Malachite sunbirds feed mostly on nectar. They do sometimes hover in front of a flowerhead to feed, like a hummingbird, but usually they perch on the flower.

Why does a toucan have such a big beak?

You can't avoid noticing a toucan's colourful, king-sized beak.

Toucans are practically more beak than body! Scientists have wondered why the beak is so large. It definitely appears to be useful for picking fruit. Toucans are heavy birds and, when they feed in the tree tops, they can't balance on the smaller branches. This would put a lot of fruit beyond reach, if it wasn't for that beak. All a toucan has to do is stretch out and help itself. A big, colourful beak also scares other birds. Toucans often raid small bird's nests for eggs and chicks. No parent bird, however outraged at the theft, is going to argue with a beak that size.

Do you know...?

Toucans are noisy birds and no one could say they have beautiful voices. They mostly make loud croaks, grunts and rattles. However, some toucans do perform a yelping song, which is a little more musical.

Why do different types of Hawaiian honeycreeper have such different beaks?

It's hard to believe that these birds are all related.

Several mllions of years ago, a type of small finch came and settled in the Hawaiian islands. Its descendants, the honeycreepers, are now spread widely over the islands, but you would never know that they are all closely related. Between the different types of honeycreeper, there is a huge range of colours, shapes, sizes and, above all, beaks. The birds evolved to take advantage of the most readily available foods. Some have short, stout beaks, typical of seed-eaters. Others are nectar-feeders, with long, thin beaks and tongues for reaching into flowers. And there are fruit-eaters with hooked beaks, like parrots.

Do you know...?

There were once many more species, or types, of honeycreeper than there are today. But many of them are now extinct. The ones that remain are under threat from diseases carried by mosquitoes. Hopefully, a way of controlling the mosquitoes will be found.

How do mousebirds hang from branches ?

Grey-brown and furry, with a long-tail – it's easy to see why these birds were given their name. Mousebirds move in a mouse-like way, too, as they scurry through branches. One of the most unusual things about them is the way they hang from branches, rather than perch on top of them. Mousebirds can do this because they have more flexible toes than most birds. They can move their toes backwards or forwards, to grip a branch any way they want. For example, they may have all four toes facing the front, or two forwards and two backwards. With such agile toes, mousebirds can even dangle from a branch with one foot while feeding on fruit or leaves held firmly in the other foot.

Two blue-naped mousebirds dangle from a branch.

Do you know...?

Mousebirds go to bed earlier and get up later than most birds. During the day, they usually take regular naps. At night, mousebirds may sleep so soundly that they can be unaware of predators until it is too late.

Why do hoatzin chicks have claws on their wings?

A hoatzin is a strange-looking bird. You could perhaps describe it as a cross between a chicken and a winged creature from the age of dinosaurs. The chicks are even stranger than their parents. They have two tiny claws on each wing. Before chicks can fly, these claws help them to pull themselves out of the nest and climb through dense branches to escape from predators. A hoatzin's nest is a rickety affair, built in a tree overhanging water. If they are in danger, the chicks sometimes jump into the water. They can swim and haul themselves back on to land with their feet and wing claws.

A hoatzin chick can clamber along branches with the help of its clawed wings.

Do you know...?

Because of the way the digestive system of a hoatzin works, it takes a long time for its food to break down. So hoatzins spend a lot of their day sitting around, waiting for their stomachs to empty.

What is a turaco?

The great blue turaco loves eating fruit and leaves.

Turacos are tree-dwelling birds, native to Africa. There are various types and they are all rather handsome birds. Many of them have richly coloured, shiny feathers. Turacos live in groups except during the breeding season, when they split up into couples to nest and raise chicks. They are extremely noisy birds and make loud croaking calls to each other across the forest. Turacos have unusually flexible feet. They can move their outer toes both forwards and backwards, giving them great ability to adjust their grip as they move along branches.

Do you know...?

The feathers of turacos take their vibrant colours from pigments that are found in no other living creature. One of the pigments is a special red and the other is green. Many turacos have bright red feathers in their wings and large areas of bright green plumage on their bodies.

What is crop milk?

Pigeon chicks, called squabs, soon grow strong on crop milk.

The nestlings of some birds are fed on a type of milk until they are old enough to eat solid food, just like human babies. A crop is a special sac, found only in a bird's body, that is used for storing food. In some birds, such as pigeons, this sac produces a nourishing fluid, known as crop milk. While pigeons are waiting for their eggs to hatch, their crops get ready to produce the 'milk'. This happens in both the parents. By the time the chicks have hatched, the parent birds have crops full of 'milk'. They regurgitate, or bring up, the crop milk into their mouths, so the chicks can take it from them. The crop then fills up again for the next meal.

Do you know...?

Young birds that are fed on crop milk grow very quickly, because the food is highly nutritious. Crop milk contains some fat and protein and a large number of vitamins.

How do mallee fowl control the temperature at which their eggs incubate?

Mallee fowl, which come from Australia, keep their eggs cosy by burying them in a mound. The male mallee fowl does the hard bit. He digs a big pit, about a metre deep and 3 metres wide, and banks up earth around it. Then the female joins in and the birds fill the pit with twigs and rotted leaves until it forms a large mound. The rotting plant material creates heat, just like in a compost heap. When the temperature of the mound reaches about 30°Celcius, the female lays her eggs in the top of it and covers them up. The male mallee fowl keeps the mound at the right temperature. He opens it up if it gets too hot and covers it again when it becomes too cool.

The female mallee fowl lays her eggs on top of a mound that she builds with her mate.

Do you know...?

Mallee fowl chicks have to dig themselves out of the mound when they hatch. Once outside, they get no help or protection from their parents, who they probably will never see. The chicks have to find all their own food and fend for themselves.

How do parrots learn to talk?

In the wild, most types of parrot don't learn to mimic sounds that are not parrot 'language'. Yet, if kept in captivity, many of them quickly start to imitate human voices and other noises. This is odd, but scientists have come up with why they do this. Each flock of wild parrots has its own particular calls, that may be slightly different from those of another flock. It is natural for each bird in a flock to learn to 'speak' in the same way as its companions. That way, the birds can recognise members of their own group. In captivity, a parrot listens to humans, not other birds. So, by following its instincts, the bird makes human sounds to become a member of a human flock!

The African grey parrot is a big chatterbox.

Do you know...?

African greys are the best talkers among parrots. In research programmes, they have been taught an amazing number of words. This research has even helped people to work out new and better ways of teaching children.

CHAPTER 6
INSECT-EATING BIRDS

Why do woodpeckers drum on trees?

The green woodpecker drums in the breeding season.

A lot of people think that when a woodpecker drums on a tree it is boring holes to look for insects. In fact, the rattling sound that echoes through the woods is 'language' that the woodpecker uses instead of its voice. When the breeding season starts, woodpeckers do bore holes in trees, to make nests. But a hole-boring woodpecker isn't drumming. A woodpecker drums to announce that it has taken possession of a tree. The sound tells strangers to go away and find their own tree! The drumming is produced by an amazingly rapid head movement. Some woodpeckers can strike a tree with their beaks more than 40 times in about two and a half seconds.

Do you know...?

The green woodpecker has an easily recognisable call. It makes a loud, ringing cry, known as a yaffle, that sounds rather like someone shrieking with laughter. 'Yaffle' is actually a common name for the green woodpecker.

How do swallows know when it is time to fly south?

In northern countries, such as Britain, everyone looks forward to seeing swallows. Their arrival from lands far in the south means that summer is here. During the warm months of the year, swallows are commonly seen around open spaces, such as farmland, swooping after the flying insects that fill the air at that time of the year. As the weather gets cooler and the days get shorter, the insects start to disappear. The swallow then knows that food is getting scarce. It's time to head for the south and a warmer climate. Swallows mass together in big groups as they prepare to start their long journey. They may line up on telegraph wires, chattering noisily to each other. Then, suddenly, they are all gone.

Time to head south.

Do you know...?

Migrating swallows fly thousands of kilometres and they like to travel together. In the autumn, large numbers of them gather at regular stopping places, such as on the Mediterranean coast. After a brief rest, the birds all move on again, still keeping together in a big group.

How do bee-eaters dig their burrows?

Bee-eaters make their nests in holes that they usually dig out for themselves. They prefer a cliff or a bank, but sometimes they burrow in flat ground. The birds tunnel into the earth with their long beaks. The burrows are normally around 7 centimetres in diameter and about a metre long. However, if bee-eaters find a really good spot where the ground is very soft and sandy, they may

The bee-eater's strong pointed beak makes a good digging tool.

Do you know...?

The male and female bee-eater work as a team to dig out their burrow. Once the soil is loosened, they kick it out of the hole with their feet. Digging a burrow keeps the pair busy for about three weeks.

dig a burrow nearly twice that length. At the end of the tunnel, the bee-eaters make a little chamber that is wider and higher than the tunnel. This is where they lay their eggs. The red-throated bee-eater, which lives in Africa, builds a ledge close to the chamber entrance to stop the eggs from rolling down the tunnel.

Why do oxpeckers ride on other animals?

On the African plains, if you dared to get close to a rhinoceros, you might see some small birds perched on the rhino's head. These birds are oxpeckers. Riding on a rhino is a dangerous thing to do. Yet the animal is glad to have passengers. Oxpeckers also hitch rides on other animals, such as antelope and hippopotamuses. Oxpeckers provide a special service. They feed on bloodsucking pests, such as ticks, that attach themselves to an animal's skin and cause irritation. The strong claws of the oxpecker help it to get a firm grip on the leathery skin of a hippo or a rhino.

Riding a rhino isn't dangerous for an oxpecker.

Do you know...?

Oxpeckers sometimes take advantage of the animals that carry them as passengers. If the animal has a wound, the oxpecker pecks at it to make it bleed. Then it feeds on the blood!

What is the use of the blue-crowned motmot's unusual tail?

This motmot is preening, not pulling bits out of its tail.

The blue-crowned motmot is just one of several South American birds called motmots. It has lovely rainbow-coloured feathers and the most extraordinary tail. This tail ends in two long, bare quills with feathery tips at the end. They look like a pair of tennis rackets.

Motmots often live in dense forests. They are secretive birds and hard to see, despite their bright colours. When a motmot sits on a branch, it keeps still, except for its tail. Anyone looking closely might see the 'rackets' swinging from side to side, like a pendulum. It is thought that the motmot swings its tail to let other motmots know it is there. That would be important in the mating season.

Do you know...?

People once thought that motmots pulled the feathery barbs out of their tails on purpose, to make them racket-shaped. In fact, the barbs are attached loosely and tend to come out when the motmot preens itself.

How can a woodcock see things at the back of its head?

You couldn't creep up behind a woodcock and take it by surprise. This bird would be able to see you coming! The woodcock's large eyes are set so high in its head that it can see in all directions, without turning its head. Because woodcocks live on the ground, they are at high risk from predators both in the air and on the ground. Having all-round vision, even when they have their heads down feeding, helps to protect the woodcock from danger.

Do you know...?

Woodcocks live on earthworms, which they search for in soft, boggy ground by probing with their long beaks. So that it can locate food easily, a woodcock stamps on the ground with its feet to get the worms moving about.

This woodcock can spot danger coming from any direction.

What makes a hoopoe's nest smell so awful?

These gorgeous birds are well known for having foul-smelling nests. Hoopoes make their nests in a variety of holes, though they especially prefer trees. When the chicks hatch, the nesting hole becomes rather cluttered with droppings and scraps of wasted food. This gets a bit smelly, but the female hoopoe cleans the nest out regularly. The awful pong is not really due to bad housekeeping, but to the hoopoe's unusual weapon of defence. Both the chicks and their mother have a scent gland near their tails. The gland contains a fluid that is said to smell like rotten meat. If the nest is approached by a predator, the birds spray out the horrible fluid. Most enemies then hastily turn and run!

Do you know...?

Hoopoes don't make their own nest holes. They may take over an abandoned woodpecker nest in a tree, or find a handy gap in a stone wall. Hoopoes are even known to make their nests in drainpipes.

Nasty smells are the hoopoe's best defence against predators!

How do barn swallows build their mud nests?

Hungry young swallows crowd together in their mud nest.

As their name suggests, barn swallows like to nest in farm buildings, either on a ledge or under a roof. They are also happy in a garage or a porch, or beneath a bridge. Their nests are carefully made cups of dried mud, that stick firmly to walls or rafters. Nest-making keeps a swallow busy for a week. The bird gathers up little pellets of mud in its beak. It builds up the pellets, one by one, into the shape of a cup. To make the nest stronger, the swallow pushes small pieces of straw or grass into the mud walls. When the cup is finished, the swallow lines it with feathers to make the inside warm and soft for the eggs.

Do you know...?

The swallow's favourite nesting places, such as barns and cow sheds, are disappearing. Many farmers have no use for such buildings and pull them down. Lack of nesting sites is one reason why swallows are not so common as they used to be.

How do woodpeckers drill holes?

Woodpeckers work in pairs to bore out a nesting hole in a tree. They choose a dead or decaying tree whenever possible, because the wood is much softer. The birds hammer away with their beaks, straight through the outer bark. Once the woodpeckers reach the inner wood, they start to bore downwards. Woodchips really start to fly as the birds hollow out a shaft inside the tree trunk. They may go down as much as 30 to 50 centimetres. Then they hack out a small chamber, where the eggs will be laid. As the woodpeckers work, they clear away a lot of the wood shavings from the hole. They will save some of the shavings and use them to make a cosy lining for their nest.

Woodpeckers prefer to drill soft, rotten wood.

Do you know...?

Why don't woodpeckers rattle their brains with all the hammering that they do? One reason is that a bird has a very small brain, which is far harder to damage than a larger brain. Also, nearly all of the impact, when a woodpecker is hammering, is below the brain area.

Why do swifts never land on the ground?

If a swift did come down to the ground, it wouldn't be able to go anywhere. Swifts have tiny legs and feet, that are completely useless for walking and hopping. A swift simply can't move around on the ground to look for food. If a predator approached, a grounded swift could have difficulty making a quick escape into the air.

Swifts almost never come down to earth.

Its short legs aren't able to give it a good push for take-off. And its long wings are difficult to flap so near to the ground. Swifts stay in the air for most of their lives. It's safer. They can catch food without ever having to land. They swoop about with their beaks gaping wide, gulping in tiny flying insects by the thousand.

Do you know...?

As well as eating on the wing, swifts mate on the wing and even appear to sleep all night on the wing. They probably sleep by drifting with their wings spread and letting the air currents hold them up.

How did the honeyguide get its name?

The honeyguide and the honey badger help each other to find food.

Honeyguides are among the wild bee's worst enemies. They not only break into bees' nests, they encourage even more destructive creatures, including humans, to join in the plunder. Honeyguides don't eat honey, but they devour bee grubs and the wax that makes up the honeycomb. When a honeyguide discovers a bees' nest, it might not be able to break it open on its own. So it draws attention to the find by fluttering about and making loud rattling calls. With luck, a honey-loving animal will follow the honeyguide and tear the bees' nest open. Then both the bird and its 'helper' can have a feast.

How come wrens have such loud voices?

Wrens are very small, round birds that are much easier to hear than they are to see. For their size, they make a lot of noise. Wrens scold furiously at the tops of their voices if they are disturbed by intruders. They are also good singers and can produce some delightful music. Wrens need to be loud to advertise themselves to other wrens. They live and nest in dense undergrowth, where a soft voice would get muffled and maybe go unnoticed. When a wren is singing to attract a mate or to announce its ownership of territory, it needs to be heard loud and clear.

The wren is a little bird with a big voice.

The wren is one of the world's best-loved birds.

Do you know...?

In the breeding season, a male common wren often builds several nests, each with a domed roof to shelter the chicks. His mate inspects all of the nests and chooses the one that suits her best.

What is courtship feeding?

A male rufous-tailed jacamar courts a female by offering her food.

Do you know...?

Courtship feeding is the male bird's way of showing the female that he is good at hunting for food. It's proof that he will make a suitable mate. The gift-giving ritual also helps to form a strong bond between the pair.

It is not only people who give each other engagement presents. Many birds do it, too. Giving gifts of food can be an important part of their courtship rituals. Antbirds are just one example. While the female antbird calls loudly, the male bobs his head at her and then rushes off to find something tasty for her to eat. He returns with his gift of an insect or grub – and somehow manages to sing with it in his beak! Then he feeds the female. Once she has eaten, the female may peck at the male's beak, as a sign that she is happy to accept him as her mate. Other birds, such as jacamars, warblers, chats and tits, also have present-giving rituals.

What is bird's nest soup?

You would have to be very rich to eat bird's nest soup. This food is considered a great delicacy in parts of Asia and it's expensive. But many people, when they know what is in the soup, don't want to try it! The soup is made from the nests of small birds called swiftlets. These birds build nests high up in caves. Some swiftlets make nests from a mixture of saliva, plants and feathers, which sets hard. Other types of swiftlet just use saliva and nothing else. Nests made only of saliva are what people use to prepare bird's nest soup.

Harvesting swiftlets' nests for soup is endangering this type of bird.

Do you know...?

Millions of swiftlet nests are found in caves and harvested every year to supply the market. There is a big demand for the nests and people will pay a lot of money for them. They may pay thousands of pounds for just 1 kilogram of swiftlet nests.

Why do host birds feed a cuckoo chick that looks nothing like their own young?

A female cuckoo snatches an egg to make room for one of her own.

Parent birds raising chicks are driven by a powerful instinct. To them, a gaping beak poking up out of a nest means a hungry baby. They just can't stop themselves from dropping food into its beak. This is why birds feed a young cuckoo that has taken over their nest. It doesn't matter that the cuckoo looks nothing like their own chicks. Indeed, the cuckoo soon grows much bigger than its hosts. That wide-open, brightly coloured mouth, known as a gape, is saying 'feed me'! To make its demands even plainer, the cuckoo keeps up a loud, begging call. The parents are quite unable to resist. They exhaust themselves trying to satisfy their ravenous foster child.

Do you know...?

After a young cuckoo has left the nest, it doesn't give up asking for food. For some weeks, it begs any passing bird to give it something to eat. Usually, instinct again forces these birds to give in to the cuckoo's pleas.

How do nuthatches walk upside down along branches?

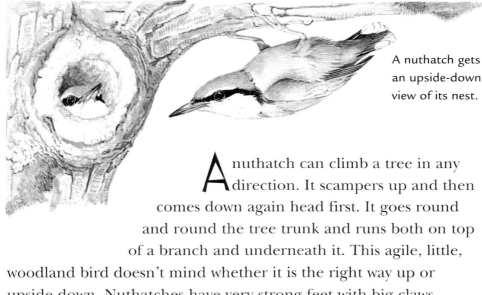

A nuthatch gets an upside-down view of its nest.

A nuthatch can climb a tree in any direction. It scampers up and then comes down again head first. It goes round and round the tree trunk and runs both on top of a branch and underneath it. This agile, little, woodland bird doesn't mind whether it is the right way up or upside down. Nuthatches have very strong feet with big claws. These feet enable the birds to cling firmly to the bark of a tree. When a nuthatch climbs, it lifts one foot further up than the other and anchors it in the bark. The bird hangs from the front foot and supports itself from the back foot. It moves rapidly about in a jerky run, first going one way and then the other.

Do you know...?

The nuthatch uses its long, pointed beak to pick insects out of narrow cracks in tree bark. It also wedges hard seeds and nuts into crevices and whacks them with its beak to break them open.

How do bee-eaters avoid getting stung?

This bee-eater has caught a large dragonfly.

If you eat bees every day, you don't want to get stung every time you catch one! A bee-eater knows how to avoid getting too many nasty jabs. A hunting bee-eater makes a short dash after a flying bee and snatches it up with a loud snap of its beak. It goes back to a perch with its prey and bangs the bee against the branch a few times to kill it. Then the bee-eater deals with the sting. The bird holds the bee near its end and rubs the insect's tail on the branch. This rubs off the sting and squeezes out the venom from the bee's poison sac. Now the prey is harmless and the bee-eater swallows it whole.

Do you know...?

Bee-eaters eat other insects besides bees and can recognise which sting and which don't. For example, hoverflies look like wasps, but don't sting. Bee-eaters swallow hoverflies without rubbing them against a branch.

How do Indian swiftlets find their way in the dark?

Indian swiftlets roost in totally dark caves, where they gather in huge colonies. This behaviour is more like that of a bat than a bird. In fact, the swiftlet can find its way in the dark just like a bat does. To avoid banging into things it can't see, the swiftlet uses a system called echolocation. As it flies, it sends out a rapid clicking call. The clicks echo back from anything in the way. And the bird can tell immediately if it needs to change direction. The echoes also stop the swiftlet from colliding with other swiftlets in the cave. But the bird's echolocation system is not as amazingly accurate as that of a bat. A swiftlet can't use echoes to locate tiny objects such as insects.

A swiftlet isn't afraid of the dark!

Do you know...?

Swiftlets hunt for flying insects by sight. Again, in a rather bat-like way, swiftlets often go out hunting after sunset, when most other birds are thinking about going to bed.

How did the wryneck get its name?

The wryneck sometimes acts like a snake!

The word 'wry' means twisted. The wryneck can twist its neck right round until its beak points to its back. The bird, which is a type of woodpecker, performs this extraordinary movement when it is threatened. If a wryneck is disturbed, it weaves and turns its neck about like a snake. It also raises the feathers on its head. As if that wasn't enough to frighten someone away, the wryneck hisses like an angry snake. Such alarming behaviour often works very well in scaring off small predators. The wryneck isn't really fierce at all. It is a secretive bird that hops quietly about in trees or on the ground, hunting for ants. The wryneck is hard to spot because its grey-brown feathers blend into its surroundings.

Do you know...?

It is said that in olden times witches used the wryneck to cast spells. Perhaps this was because the way the bird behaved looked so strange. People may have thought that it had special powers.

Why is there a fan on the Pacific royal flycatcher's head?

Most of the time, as it goes about its business, the Pacific royal flycatcher looks like a very ordinary bird. Its plumage is brown and buff. A few bright feathers might just be visible on its head. But when the flycatcher wants to be noticed, it has a surprise in store. It raises a crest of feathers on its head that normally stays hidden. A spectacular fan in scarlet, blue and black springs open, transforming the dull bird into something amazing. Royal flycatchers don't show off their fans very often. They usually display them on special occasions, such as when they are courting or competing with rivals.

Do you know...?

As well as having a fan on its head, the Pacific royal flycatcher has magnificent whiskers around the base of its beak. These whiskers act as an insect trap, stopping the bird's insect prey from dodging its gaping beak.

A gorgeous fan opens up on this flycatcher's head.

How do woodpeckers catch their prey?

There are many different types of woodpecker. Between them, they have lots of ways of catching the insects that are the main part of their diet. Often, a woodpecker just picks up an insect from a branch or a leaf. To reach insects hiding in the tree bark, a woodpecker pokes around with its beak. If insects have burrowed into the tree, the woodpecker drills holes in the wood and uses its tongue to hook out its prey.

Do you know...?

If a woodpecker can't see any insects on a tree, it tries listening for them instead. The bird gives a sharp rap with its beak to get the insects scurrying about under the bark. A woodpecker can hear even the tiniest movement.

A woodpecker goes grubbing around for food.

The green woodpecker has a very special tongue. It is exceptionally long and is sticky. This makes it particularly good for catching ants. The bird uses its tongue to dig deep down into an ant nest and lap up all the ants and grubs that it finds there.

How did the antbird get its name?

The birds grouped under this name are forest birds of all sorts. You may think that they eat nothing but ants. But antbirds don't usually eat any ants at all! They take their name from some birds in the group that have the habit of following swarms of ferocious ants, known as army ants. Every so often, the ants swarm, marching in columns through the forest. They devour any small creatures, such as other insects, that cross their path. As these little creatures scurry to get out of the way, the antbirds move in, snapping up the prey that escapes the terrible army.

Thanks to the marching ants, this antbird has caught an insect.

Do you know...?

Antbirds include antpittas, antshrikes, ant-thrushes, antwrens and more. Not all are closely related. The birds that follow ants actually keep a regular watch on ant colonies to see if they are ready to swarm.

How do cuckoos disguise their eggs?

Before a female cuckoo lays an egg in another bird's nest, she has to do some careful planning. First, it is important for her to find a type of bird whose eggs are very like her own. Cuckoo eggs vary in pattern and colour, so the female has to be sure of a near match. Once the cuckoo has chosen the foster parents for her egg, she watches their nest until the first eggs have been laid. The instant the parent birds leave the nest unattended, the cuckoo goes into action. In just 10 seconds, she grabs an egg from the nest with her beak, replaces it with her own egg and flies off. When the parent birds return, they usually fail to notice anything odd.

A female cuckoo with a stolen egg.

Do you know...?

A cuckoo chick wants the nest to itself. After it hatches, the chick pushes out any other eggs, or even other chicks. It lifts a victim onto its back and tips it out, over the edge of the nest.

Spot the cuckoo's egg! It's the larger one on the left of each pair.

How can I help baby robins?

Baby robins never stop asking for food.

Robins are happy to rear their young close to where people live. You might see a nest near your home. If one turns up in a garage or a garden shed, be sure to leave any doors open so that the parent robins can go in and out to feed

Do you know...?

Almost anywhere makes a suitable nesting site for robins, as long as it is fairly well hidden. As well as using purpose-built boxes, robins have raised families in old kettles, flower pots, drainpipes and dumped cars!

their brood. Baby robins are permanently hungry. You can give their parents a hand by leaving out suitable food in a safe place, such as on a bird table. Mealworms, which you can buy in a pet shop, are best. If you own a cat, remember that cats chase birds! Put a bell on your pet's collar to warn the parent robins of danger.

CHAPTER 7
OMNIVOROUS BIRDS

What are perching birds?

The familiar robin is a perching bird.

Perching birds is a general term that describes a huge number of different types of bird that all have certain things in common. Most obviously, perching birds perch! They always have four toes that are shaped for holding on to narrow branches. All perching birds live on land, so they never have webbed feet, like ducks. Many of the most commonly seen birds, such as blackbirds, starlings, crows, sparrows and robins are perching birds. Nearly every country in the world has perching birds. They are missing only in places like Antarctica, where conditions are extreme.

Do you know...?

The scientific word for the perching bird group is Passeriformes. These birds include the best singers, often referred to separately as songbirds. They also include such wonderful musicians as thrushes and skylarks.

Why do great tits sing louder in town than in the country?

The great tit is both a town and a country bird.

Great tits are among many birds that are as happy to live in towns and cities as they are to live in the country. Scientists have carried out some interesting research into urban great tits. They have discovered that birds living in noisy areas tend to sing louder than those who prefer peaceful woodlands. The roar of traffic and hooting cars drowns out the lower notes of a great tit's songs. Birds need their songs to be heard because they are an important way of claiming territory. So town tits sing their songs louder to carry above the traffic noise. This ensures that any rivals for territory get the message loud and clear – keep away!

Do you know...?

Great tits will visit a garden if they know there is a good supply of food. These birds love to swing on a bird feeder full of peanuts or seeds. They are often seen feeding in company with other small birds, such as blue tits.

Why are chickadees often so tame?

Chickadees are as popular in American gardens as robins are in British ones. Because people love to have chickadees around, they often put out food for them, especially in winter. As a result, chickadees become accustomed to being near houses. They return again and again for a decent meal when other food is scarce. A well-stocked bird table can be a lifesaver for chickadees in cold weather. These birds like fatty foods, such as bacon rind. They also enjoy seeds of various kinds. Often they take seeds from a bird-feeder and store them elsewhere, such as in the bark of a tree. Chickadees can become bold and, like robins, hop quite close to a person who is keeping very still and quiet.

The black-capped chickadee is one of America's best-loved birds.

Do you know...?

The black-capped chickadee is the most common garden visitor. The Carolina chickadee of the southern states doesn't have to face such cold winters, so it is not so likely to look for food put out by people. There are also chickadees that live in mountain forests.

Which bird is the best mimic?

Parrots are good mimics, but many people think hill mynahs are better. The mynahs come from India, Thailand, Malaysia and other South-east Asian countries. In the wild, hill mynahs mimic only other mynahs. But many people keep them as pets because they are easily tamed. Captive mynahs are brilliant at imitations of people's voices. They say words more clearly than parrots and can sound amazingly like a person talking. If captive mynahs are not encouraged to talk, they imitate other sounds, such as clanking buckets and shutting doors.

The hill mynah does clever imitations of human voices.

Do you know...?

The common starling is another good mimic. It doesn't copy human speech but it imitates the sounds of other birds. A starling's song contains various notes and snippets of music that it has borrowed from different birds.

What makes feathers iridescent?

A hummingbird's feathers keep changing colour as it moves.

Do you know...?

The colours of birds are also produced by pigments in their feathers. Black and brown are the most common colours. Some pigments, such as green, are rare.

Iridescence is the lovely effect that you see when rainbow colours appear to play over a bird's feathers. For example, one minute a bird looks black, then it moves and the feathers shine blue or green or maybe purple. Birds such as starlings and hummingbirds have iridescent plumage. The effect is caused by the way their feathers are made. Each feather has a main stem, or shaft. Tiny, feathery barbs branch off the shaft and even tinier bits of feather, called barbules, branch off the barbs. In many birds, the barbules have hooks that join them together. In iridescent feathers, the barbules don't join together and they are twisted. Light rays falling on twisted barbules are reflected in different colours.

Why do starlings form such huge flocks?

Do you know...?

Starlings are welcome on farmland in spring and summer because they eat insect pests that damage crops. In autumn and winter, starlings are not so popular. The insects have gone, so they raid grain stores and orchards.

Starlings normally stick together in enormous flocks. They wheel through the air in tight formation. If one lands, within seconds they've all landed. If one takes off again, the sky is instantly filled with birds. Starlings are very sociable. As soon as the young birds leave the nest, they join up with other starlings. Mega-sized flocks occur when many separate groups of starlings all gather in the same place. This happens when one group finds a good food supply. In no time, wave after wave of starlings come to share the feast. The largest flocks are seen in the evening, when starlings all roost together.

Thousands of starlings turn the sky black.

Why do waxwings appear in great numbers every few years?

You are more likely to see a waxwing in winter.

Like many birds, waxwings migrate. They breed in one place in summer and fly south in winter to find food and shelter. Most migrating birds appear in the same sites year after year. Waxwings do it differently. When these birds leave their summer grounds they don't fly south on autopilot to a regular wintering place. They take any route that might lead to a good food supply. When they find food, they stop. Suddenly, the place is full of waxwings. In spring, they may go back to a new breeding area. The following winter, they take yet another route. That explains why birdwatchers can't expect to see waxwings at the same site every year.

Do you know...?

Waxwings don't alter their migration routes just for a nice change. They do it because in any one area the berries they eat can be plentiful one year and scarce the next. The waxwings are simply looking for the nearest source of food.

How do dunnocks compete for mates?

A dunnock may have just one mate, or several.

Life for a dunnock in the breeding season gets very complicated. These birds have several ways of matching themselves up with partners. Some dunnocks form pairs and set up a nest as a twosome. However, sometimes a male mates with two females. He must defend both of them against rivals. Things can also happen the other way round. A female might form a partnership with two males. Naturally, the males have a few arguments about this. In time, one male becomes the senior mate and the other accepts a more lowly position. They link territories and both defend the female. In the most confusing arrangement of all, several males share the defence of several females.

Do you know...?

Female dunnocks that have more than one mate are most likely to rear chicks successfully. The males share the feeding and protection of the chicks between them, so the youngsters have a good chance of surviving.

Why do birds carry their chicks' droppings away from the nest?

A nestful of chicks means a lot of poo! Not all birds keep spotless nests, but most of them remove the droppings regularly. It would be easy for a parent bird just to pick up the poo and drop it over the edge of the nest. But many birds carry the droppings well away from the nest. It sounds a chore, but it is a sensible safety measure. Predators can pick up the scent of bird droppings. The smell tells them that there are baby birds around. Moving the droppings lessens the danger of chicks being discovered.

Do you know...?

Some baby birds are very good at keeping their nests clean and tidy. Among these are hornbill chicks, which are brought up in a hole in a tree. When they need to poo, they stick their behinds out of the entrance to the hole!

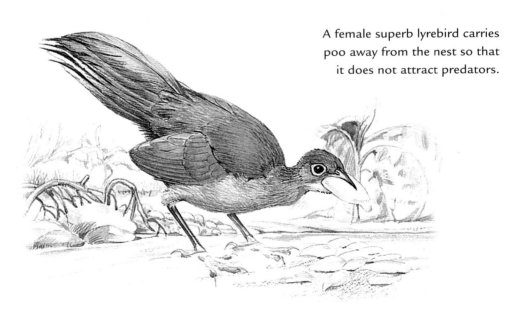

A female superb lyrebird carries poo away from the nest so that it does not attract predators.

Why does the early bird catch the worm?

Do you know...?

Worms fight back when birds grab hold of them! They have tiny bristles along their bodies that catch in the soil. This is why birds often have to pull with all their strength in order to drag a worm out of the ground.

Worms wake up early. They are most likely to be moving about near the surface of the soil first thing in the morning. Birds that love worms for breakfast have to be up in good time to catch them. Worm-eaters include robins, blackbirds and thrushes. These birds can see well in the sometimes dull and misty light just after dawn. On a worm hunt, they hop along the ground, pausing every now and then to cock their heads and listen. Their sharp ears can detect the movement of a worm just beneath their feet. They make a quick pounce with their beaks and haul the worm out. It's often quite a struggle as the bird backs away and the worm seems to stretch out longer and longer.

This thrush has caught a fine worm for breakfast.

Why are robins the gardener's friend?

The handle of a garden fork makes a good perch for a robin.

Do you know...?

In cold weather, when grubs are scarce, you can entice robins into a garden by putting out food on a bird table. Natural foods, such as mealworms, are best. But robins will also eat scraps, such as bits of cheese or breadcrumbs.

A gardener who has a visiting robin is lucky. Many of the grubs that munch their way through someone's treasured plants are among the robin's favourite foods. Robins are not shy of people and are common in both town and country gardens all year round. They like areas that are not too overgrown, so a tidy garden is perfect for them. Robins search for food by watching from a perch or by hopping along the ground. They can be quite bold, coming close to a gardener to see if anything that is good to eat is being dug up. It is also nice to have a robin about because the bird's bright red breast makes it such an attractive bird. Robins are musical, too. Their sweet song brightens up any gardener's day.

Why do oropendolas build such strange nests?

In a tropical jungle, the last thing you would expect to see is a lot of long, woven bags dangling from a tree. They are the nests of oropendolas, birds that are related to the American blackbird.

An oropendola's nest can be up to 1.5 metres long. It has an entrance at the top and the eggs are laid in the bottom of the bag. These marvellous nests provide good protection against predators. Even if a predator could climb up trees, it would have great difficulty reaching any eggs or chicks. This bird makes its nest with plant fibres, which it first ties firmly to a branch. Then it weaves the bag. Day by day, the nest gets longer and longer.

The nests of an oropendola colony hang like washing on a line.

Do you know...?

Many other types of bird, besides the oropendola, make woven nests. There is actually a big group of birds that is known as the weavers. They create beautiful nests, using a wide variety of materials, from fine grasses to bark torn into strips with their beaks.

Why are **common** starlings so widespread?

You are never far from a starling!

There are millions of starlings in Europe, America, Asia, South Africa and even Australia and New Zealand. Starlings first lived in Europe and spread from there, mainly because they are good at living near humans. Thousands of years ago, Europeans started clearing forests to make farmland. The starlings loved cleared land. They travelled beyond Europe to take advantage of new farmland everywhere. In some countries, starlings were released on purpose. Starlings were taken to New Zealand to help control insect pests.

Do you know...?

In 1890, 60 starlings were released in New York's Central Park. The descendants of these few birds are now spread across nearly the whole of North America. There are said to be about 200 million of them!

Why do some birds sit on ant nests?

A blue jay squashes an ant into its wing feathers.

Birds belonging to the crow family, including jays and magpies, have an odd habit called anting. To go anting, a bird sits on top of an ant colony and shakes its wings and tail. The disturbed ants rush to defend their nest against the intruder. Ants on the attack squirt a chemical, called formic acid, from their jaws. This acid is sprayed into the bird's feathers. Formic acid can give you a painful sting but, strangely, the bird is not at all bothered. No one is sure why birds go anting. But scientists think that formic acid may keep bloodsucking pests out of the birds' plumage.

How do thrushes open snails?

Do you know...?

Thrushes often go back to the same snail-smashing stone over and over again. This lunch spot is easy to spot because the ground around the stone becomes littered with bits of shell.

One of the song thrush's favourite foods is a snail. You will know that as soon as you try to touch a snail it disappears into its shell. And if a snail senses that a thrush is near, it immediately does its vanishing act. If the thrush wants a meal, it has to work for it. The bird picks up the snail shell by the rim and carries it to a flat stone or rock. Then it proceeds to bash the shell against the stone. Before long, the shell cracks and the thrush pulls out a juicy snail to eat. If you are in a garden or a park, you can sometimes hear the 'tap-tap' of a thrush breaking open a snail shell.

A thrush hammers open a snail.

Which are the smartest birds?

Do you know...?

Crows sometimes hide food, such as acorns, in special stores, to save it for times when there is little around to eat. They have very good memories and are usually able to find their secret larders at a later date.

The jackdaw is a smart bird.

Most birds are pretty clever. They have to be to survive. But the geniuses of the bird world are the crow family. They include ravens, jackdaws and jays. Crows are most likely to use their brain power when there's food around. They eat almost anything and will do almost anything to get it. Crows have learned how to break the shells of nuts and shellfish by dropping them on to a hard surface from exactly the right height. They sometimes use tools, such as twigs, to hook out hard-to-get insects from tight cracks. Crows are crafty at raiding people's rubbish bins and are even known to open picnic boxes.

Do birds play?

The toucan is always ready for a good game.

Birds often take time out for a bit of fun. The toucans of South America love wrestling matches. One seizes another by the beak and they tug backwards and forwards. These birds also chase one another. One of their favourite games is playing ball, which involves tossing fruit to each other with their beaks. Another bird with a sense of mischief is the kea, a parrot from New Zealand. Kea games include wheeling about in the air, rolling in snow and sliding down slopes.

Do you know...?

The raven looks like a solemn bird in its black plumage, but it knows how to enjoy itself. Ravens take great delight in performing aerial somersaults and in flying upside down. They sometimes deliberately drop a twig just for the pleasure of swooping down to catch it.

How do magpies acquire territory?

A magpie without territory doesn't easily acquire somewhere of its own. If it tries to move in on another bird's patch, the resident bird puts up an angry resistance. If the intruder patrols the territorial boundary, looking for a chance to slip in,

Do you know...?

If a female magpie is not satisfied with the territory she shares with a mate, she gets divorced! She leaves her mate and looks for another magpie with a bigger territory, where food is more plentiful.

A magpie doesn't allow intruders on to its territory and will fight to defend its space.

the resident bird shadows it menacingly. The potential intruder would be wise to make itself scarce. If not, the resident magpie will attack with beak and claws. A magpie may gain some territory if one bird of a resident pair dies. In this case, the newcomer may move in on the same day. Young magpies can win territory by forming a gang. With a 'gangleader' at their head, they bully resident birds. Every now and then, the gang is successful.

Why are people superstitious about crows?

In any country where there are crows, there seem to be some odd very beliefs about them. There was once a superstition that if a crow flew past a window, it meant that someone in the house was about to die. Native American warriors used to put crow feathers in their headdresses.

In the past, many people thought that crows brought ill fortune.

Do you know...?

Ravens, which are very large members of the crow family, are always kept at the Tower of London. There is a story from long ago warning that if the ravens leave the Tower, the monarchy will fall. Even today, no one is taking any chances!

This was because they believed that the birds had control over life and death. Magpies have long been linked with the Devil or with witchcraft. An ancient rhyme says of magpies that 'one is for sorrow'. In the past, if someone saw a lone magpie, he or she was advised to spit three times in order to avoid bad luck!

How do cocks-of-the-rock go courting?

The male cock-of-the-rock has spectacular feathers.

The forests of South America are scenes of some amazing ceremonies when cocks-of-the-rock go courting. There are two types of cock-of-the-rock – the Guianan type and the Andean type.

The males hold courting displays at special sites called leks. But Guianan birds and Andean birds have different ways of trying to impress the females. A Guianan bird performs mostly at ground level. In front of a female, he fans out his wings and tail. To show off his fancy headdress, he turns his head sideways. While this is going on, rival males try to shoo the female away. Andean birds perform up in the trees. The male faces the female, because his big crest looks better from this angle. Rival Andean males are not rude enough to try and spoil the show.

Do you know...?

Male cocks-of-the-rock have gorgeous orange and black plumage and large fan-like crests on their heads. The females are dark olive-brown and have smaller crests. This duller plumage helps to make the females less visible when they are sitting on their nests.

How do birds sing?

A small bird can make a big noise!

Anyone who hears the 'dawn chorus' knows how wonderful birdsong sounds. A songbird's throat is made specially to produce music. In our throats, we have a voice box, or larynx, containing vocal cords. The cords vibrate when air passes over them and make sounds. We use our mouths to shape the sounds. A bird's larynx doesn't have vocal cords. But birds have an organ called a syrinx. This contains membranes that are tightened and loosened by muscles. A bird uses its syrinx to make different notes.

Do you know...?

Birds sing for all kinds of reasons. One of the most important is to announce to the world that they are in possession of territory. Some birds sing to attract mates and a few, such as blackbirds, sing duets together.

Why do skylarks sing in flight?

A skylark's song is often heard coming loud and clear from the sky, even if the bird cannot be seen. Skylarks are tiny and not very noticeable in their brown and buff plumage. It is the male skylark that sings so beautifully. When he is courting, his song is meant to draw the attention of females. And when a pair of skylarks have settled down to nest, the male still goes on singing.

Do you know...?

To finish off a song flight, the skylark comes back down to earth with a flourish. Often the bird descends in a rapid spiral. Sometimes, though, he drops suddenly like an open parachute.

This time, the song is his way of keeping rivals away from his territory. On a song flight, the skylark shoots up high into the air, until he is nearly invisible. Once up there, he hovers, sometimes for many minutes, singing without a pause.

A skylark usually sings on the wing.

How do umbrellabirds display their strange plumage?

An umbrellabird looks as if it is wearing a scarf and carrying an umbrella.

There can't be many birds in an Amazonian forest much stranger than an umbrellabird. It has the most extraordinary topknot, that really does look like a black umbrella. And hanging beneath its throat, like a scarf, is a long, feathery wattle. The male umbrellabird uses these decorations frequently for a weird piece of showing off. First, he perches at the top of a tree. He leans forwards, letting the 'umbrella' flop over his eyes and beak. Then he raises the feathers on his wattle. He straightens up slowly, then suddenly thrusts out his neck and lets out a loud cry. The point is to let other birds know where he is.

Do you know...?

The male umbrellabird's deafening bellow can be heard over long distances. He makes this noise by filling up an air sac in his throat and letting the air out with a rush.

Why is the northern mockingbird such a popular state emblem?

The mockingbird has a wonderful singing voice.

Do you know...?

Because of their singing, many mockingbirds were once captured and sold as cagebirds. In some places, they became quite scarce. Today, most pet mockingbirds are bred in captivity and are rarely taken from the wild.

Mockingbirds are common all over the United States, where they also appear as the emblem for five states. They have long been popular because of their wonderful singing. The mockingbird's song is quite complicated. These birds are good mimics and also insert song notes copied from other types of bird. In addition, mockingbirds often mimic other sounds, such as the human voice. A mockingbird continues to add new notes to its song throughout its life. Over the years, a bird's song may acquire as many as 200 different sounds. Mockingbirds sing to attract mates and to defend their territory. Like nightingales, they sing at night.

OMNIVIROUS BIRDS

Why don't birds pee?

I n our bodies, the kidneys filter out waste from the blood and mix it with water to make urine, which is then stored in the bladder. When your bladder is full, you feel uncomfortable and you have to go and pee. Birds don't have a urinary system like ours, so they don't pee. If a bird had a bladder full of pee, the weight would make it difficult to fly. Waste from a bird's kidneys go down a tube to the end the bird's gut. The bird then passes watery waste out of its body along with any solid waste from its digestive system.

Seabirds can't pee, but they produce vast amounts of poo!

Do you know...?

Droppings from birds that live in big colonies, like gulls, can build up into enormous piles. Known as guano, this stuff is full of nutrients that are good for the soil. In many parts of the world, guano is regarded as a valuable fertiliser.

How has skylark song inspired poets and composers?

A skylark is hard to see on the ground.

For hundreds of years, the skylark's singing has inspired poetry and music. The most famous poem about a skylark was written by Percy Bysshe Shelley in the early 19th century. He called the skylark a 'blithe spirit' (meaning a joyful spirit). Composers have tried to imitate the skylark's song. They have also used musical notes to represent the bird's soaring flight. In 1914, the composer Ralph Vaughan Williams wrote music in which the sound of a violin makes listeners think of a skylark in the air.

Do you know...?

Skylarks often nest on farmland, where they eat grain and feed their chicks on insects. But modern farming methods have reduced the skylarks' food supply. As a result, there are fewer skylarks than there used to be.